The Final Chapter of World Missions:

Releasing the Hosts of the Eleventh Hour

The Final Chapter of World Missions:

Releasing the Hosts of the Eleventh Hour

BEAT JOST

William Carey Library
Pasadena, California
www.WCLBooks.com

The Final Chapter of World Missions: Releasing the Hosts of the 11th Hour

Cover design: Melissa Dorr and Amanda Valloza

Published by William Carey Library
1605 E. Elizabeth Street
Pasadena, California 91104
www.wclbooks.com

William Carey Library is a Ministry of the
U.S. Center for World Mission, Pasadena, California.

ISBN 0-87808-346-4

Printed in the United States of America

Contents

INTRODUCTION

"Forget the former things; do not dwell on the past. See, I am doing a new thing! Now it springs up; do you not perceive it? I am making a way in the desert and streams in the wasteland."

(Isaiah 43:18-19)

"Look at the nations and watch - and be utterly amazed. For I am going to do something in your days that you would not believe, even if you were told."

(Habakkuk 1:5)

"See, I am doing a new thing" – God, the Lord of the harvest, has seen that the current missions workforce will not be able to fulfill his commission. They are working hard, making many sacrifices, and bringing in a fair amount of the harvest. But there are still thousands of fields ripe for harvest and not enough workers. Therefore God in his sovereignty has chosen to create something new in the history of missions: he has prepared hosts of new workers to bring in his harvest.

"Now it springs up" – Now, at the beginning of the 21st century, these hosts of new workers are appearing. These new workers have already begun working in the harvest, but only now are they ready to be unleashed in countless numbers. Our generation is privileged to witness the beauty of God's plan and participate in it.

"Do you not perceive it?" – Do we see his "new thing?" Do we perceive these new hosts that the Lord has appointed to fulfil his mission? Are we willing to work with the Holy Spirit in a new way, or are we clinging to the past?

World history and missions history are building toward the climax that the Bible foretells in Revelation. While the world slides into chaos and anarchy, the Lord is preparing his church as the bride for the wedding feast, in which all nations, tribes and tongues will take part, and missions history will finally come to its closure.

This paper will use the analogy that Jesus used in Matthew 20 to describe the different workers in the harvest. In this parable, Jesus describes a landowner who hires workers at different times of the day to harvest in his vineyard. Near the end of the day, the harvest is not yet complete, so he brings in many new workers – the workers of the 11th hour – to finish the harvest.

This paper will examine these hosts of workers for the end times more closely. Chapter 1 addresses what they look like, and how they can adapt to an ever-changing world. Chapter 2 proposes strategic principles that will make them most effective. Chapter 3 discusses how the other harvesters should partner with them, including the issue of funding where appropriate. Chapter 4 describes visions for completing the harvest.

Chapter 1

The Workers of the 11th Hour of World Mission

1.1 The Workers: The hosts of the 11th hour have a new face

In the 20th century the Christian world experienced radical changes, which the average church member in the West is not aware of. In many Western countries, church membership is declining, while other parts of the world are experiencing absolutely amazing awakening and revival.

For example, the worldwide Anglican Church is experiencing dramatic growth in Africa but significant decline in Europe and North America.

> Growth since 1970 in various provinces of the Anglican Communion: Ghana, +136%; Kenya, +432%; Nigeria, +518%; Sudan, +633%; Uganda, +570%; United States, -28%; Britain, -14%; Canada, -33%; Scotland, -44%.[1]

The church has become more diverse and its numerical center has shifted from North America and Europe (the "Global North") to Latin America, Africa, and Asia (the "Global South"). At the beginning of the 20th century, 95% of all Christians lived in the Global North. Today, 80% of all Christians live in the Global South, and this numerical shift is increasing, as highlighted by Patrick Johnstone:

> The real growth has been in Latin America, Africa and Asia....In 1960, non-Western Evangelicals were half as numerous as Western Evangelicals. But by 2000 they will be four times more numerous, and if such growth rates continue, in the year 2010 they will be seven times more numerous.[2]

This fact has dramatic implications for world missions. In the next few years, the "white faces" of the Global North will be joined and complemented by the "black, yellow and brown faces" of the Global South. In the year 2025, four out of five missionaries will come from the Global South. To reach the remaining unreached people groups, the church in the West must move into the role of a partner for specialised tasks and mandates. The work of the harvest will largely be done by missionaries of the Global South: the hosts of the 11th hour.

Robert Reeve says: "Matthew 20:1-16 is a prophetic parable for these new realities of world missions."[3]

In this parable of the workers in the vineyard, God is looking for men and women who are called by him into his vineyard. He is the Lord of the harvest and calls workers into his harvest field.

If we look at the history of missions, we can relate the five phases of missions to the five groups of workers in this parable. The workers "in the morning" are the missionaries of the Old Testament. The workers of the "third hour" are the missionaries of the New Testament. The workers of the "sixth hour" are the missionaries of the 4th to 18th centuries. The workers of the "ninth hour" are the missionaries of the 19th and 20th centuries. The workers of the "eleventh hour" are the missionaries of the 21st century – the final era of world missions.

1.1.1 "Early in the morning..." – Missionaries of the Old Testament

> For the Kingdom of heaven is like a landowner who went out early in the morning to hire men to work in his vineyard. He agreed to pay a denarius for the day and sent them into this vineyard (Mt. 20:1-2).

Missions is not a modern invention, nor is it a Great Commission that began only in the New Testament. Missions began in the Garden of Eden, when God called Adam after the fall: "Where are you?" (Gen. 3:9).

Missions begins in the heart of God, with his longing to restore the relationship with man. Therefore missions began at the Fall – in the very moment when the relationship between God and man broke off because of sin.

Therefore, since the Fall, he again and again called people into his service to show to all nations his offer for forgiveness and restoration.

The prophets of the Old Testament that were called by God to the nations were the first missionaries. From a missiological perspective, they were commissioned by God "early in the morning":

- *Noah* was called and used by God to preach to a decadent world that the only way to redemption was through repentance (2 Peter 2:5).
- *Abraham* was called by God out of a pagan environment to become a blessing for all the families of the world (Gen. 12:1-3).
- *Jonah* was sent by God with a message of repentance and hope to the pagan city of Nineveh (Jonah 1:1-2; 3:1-4).
- *Israel* as a nation was called by God to be his people and to shine as a light to the nations (Isaiah 43:1.10).

1.1.2. "The third hour..." – Missionaries of the New Testament

> About the third hour he went out and saw others standing in the marketplace doing nothing. He told them, 'You also go and work in my vineyard, and I will pay you whatever is right.' So they went (Mt. 20:3-5a).

Jesus came to earth to ultimately solve the problem of sin and restore our relationship with God. He called to himself co-workers that would live with him and share his message with others.

He first called twelve disciples, then seventy-two, and finally sent all his disciples to all nations on earth to make disciples.

The apostles, prophets, and evangelists of the NT were the workers of the 3rd hour.

In the Palestinian culture of Jesus' days, the 3rd hour would correspond to 9 am our time. The workers that were engaged at 9 a.m. were ready for hard work. They might not have been very numerous, but they were full of power and achieved a lot in a short amount of time. We cannot call the workers of the 3rd hour a host, but they were an extremely useful and powerful group.

1.1.3. "The sixth hour…" – Missionaries of the 4th to 18th Centuries

"He went out again about the sixth hour" (Mt. 20:5b).

The sixth hour corresponds to noon. It is hot, progress is slow, and there are very few workers willing to be hired.

This was the situation of Christianity from the 4th to the 18th century. A few individuals were ready to work in the harvest fields. Some examples are Boniface, who evangelised all of Germany and the Netherlands in the 8th century, and Anchaire, who did the same in Scandinavia. Lull was the first to do so among Muslims in Tunisia in the 13th century. Other missionaries such as Xavier or Ricci (16th century) even worked in places such as India, China, and Japan.

During that long period, there were a few shining examples of workers, who wholeheartedly and devotedly worked in the vineyard. Overall, though, the church failed miserably in terms of mission during that era.

What were the causes for this?

In the edict of Milan, in 313 AD, Emperor Constantine granted the Christian church religious freedom. Later rulers continued to grant the church privileged status, until Theodosius I in 380 AD passed an edict declaring Christianity the official state religion of the Roman Empire.[4]

The state was now no longer persecutor, but a friend of the church. World missions and evangelism lost their priority position and took on a marginal role in the following centuries. Missions lapsed into a mere welcoming gesture for heathen peoples into the now mostly nominal church.

Although this era was a time of darkness for world missions, God has never been without witnesses, and some godly men and women set out to reach a few unreached peoples and nations.

1.1.4. "The ninth hour…" – Missionaries of the 19th and 20th Centuries

> He went out again about…the ninth hour and did the same thing (Mt. 20:5b).

The 9th hour of world missions is the era of the so-called modern world missions that began at the end of the 18th century.

The era of modern mission began with William Carey (1761-1834). The following 200 years were full of exceptional advances in many parts of the world. Thousands, even millions of people of all nations came into contact with the gospel and churches were planted all over the world. By the year 2000, there were no countries in the world without a church.

We can divide the era of modern world missions in four phases (adapted from Ralph Winter's model,[5] see table on next page).

Despite the tremendous progress of modern missions, there are still thousands of peoples completely without Christian messengers, without the Bible in their own language, and without churches.

Therefore the Lord of the harvest goes out again, to enlist more workers.

1.1.5. "The eleventh hour…" – Missionaries of the Final Era of World Missions

> About the eleventh hour, he went out and found still others standing around. He asked them, 'Why have you been standing here all day long doing nothing?' 'Because no one has hired us'

Phase	Time span	Vision	Method	Characteristics
1	1792-1910	To the coastlands	Pioneering	➢ Political Context: Colonial times – missionaries are often connected to colonial masters. ➢ Leaders are pioneers and do most of the work on their own. ➢ No existing churches on the mission field. ➢ Contextualization is disdained and unknown.
2	1865-1980	To the Inland areas	Parenting	➢ Political Context: Colonial era is nearing its end, rise of nationalism. ➢ First indigenous churches established ➢ Local leaders are trained, but leadership is still firmly in the hands of foreign missionaries. ➢ Church planting happens through foreign missionaries.
3	1934-1990	To the unreached peoples 10/40 Window	Partnering	➢ Political Context: Transition to self-government. ➢ Local, well educated leaders take leadership positions. ➢ Churches are increasingly planted without the help of foreign missionaries. ➢ Local Christians show rising interest in missions among unreached people groups. ➢ Work among unreached people groups becomes the focus of Western missionaries.
4	1990 – Fulfilment	*All* unreached peoples Mega Cities	Participating	➢ Political Context: Rising nationalism and self-confidence in the Global South. ➢ Real partnership between national and foreign missionaries as equal partners. ➢ The remaining unreached people groups are reached through cooperation. ➢ Contextualization is normal and normative. ➢ Work of western missionaries: In already reached people groups: specialised work and training; among unreached people groups: wherever possible church planting in true partnership with indigenous missionaries. ➢ Western missionary doesn't appear as superior, but as co-worker and friend.

Table 1: The four phases of modern mission

> they answered, he said to them 'You also go and work in my vineyard (Mt. 20:6-7).

Although the workers of the 9th hour worked tremendously hard and brought in an important *part* of the harvest, the Lord of the harvest has seen that it is impossible for them to bring in the whole harvest. If they continue working at the same speed that they have until now, they won't be able to reach the unreached peoples with the gospel.

> Thanks for the advances in the last 200 years – but we don't have another 200 years. In these last hours we must work just as much as in all the hours before put together.[6]

The workers of the 11th hour know that they do not have much time left. The verses in Matthew's gospel indicate the urgency of their task.

> A special emphasis is put on the events of the eleventh hour, the time between 4 and 5 o'clock. Recruiting at such late hour was very unusual. Once again the urgency of the work is shown. In John 9:4, Jesus talks about the same harvest urgency: 'as long as it is day, we must do the work of him who sent me. Night is coming, when no one can work.'.... That also is the reason why the Lord recruits so late: his work needs be done soon and unconditionally.[7]

For this urgent work, God has prepared new hosts. Their appearance differs from the others. They work with different strategies and methods. They are more courageous and flexible, and they are powerfully anointed with God's Spirit.

These new hosts have a new appearance. The workers of the 9th hour were mostly white. The hosts of the 11th hour won't have a white majority. Even though there will be white faces in it (every church is called to mission), it will mainly be black (Sub-Saharan Africa), brown (Latin-America/Asia) and yellow (Asia).

The host of the 11th hour is larger than any host previous to it. The Chinese house church movement alone plans to send 100,000 missionaries in the next years. Many other churches of the Global South have similarly ambitious visions.

We can summarize the first chapter in the table below:

	Early morning	3rd Hour	6th Hour	9th Hour	11th Hour
Era	Old Testament	Pentecost– 4th	4th – 18th	19th – 20th	21st
Origin of the workers	Jewish	Mostly Jewish	Mostly European	Mostly Global North (North America and Europe)	Mostly Global South (Latin America, Africa and Asia)
God's commission	Blessings for all people; light of the nations.	Make disciples of all nations	Make disciples of all nations	Make disciples of all nations	Make disciples of all nations
Primary emphasis	Certain nations, mostly Israel	The ends of the Roman Empire	Europe	All nations	All peoples
Place of worship	Altars, Tabernacle, Temple	Houses of the believers	Cathedrals	Church buildings	Houses of the believers

Table 2: The eras and workers of mission history

1.2. THE TIME: THE WORKERS OF THE 11TH HOUR LIVE IN THE FINAL HOUR OF WORLD HISTORY

The 20th century has brought about massive historical changes. The time span of 1945-1970 revolutionized the non-Western world. Ralph Winter calls this span of time "the unbelievable twenty-five years" and explains:

> By 1945, Europeans had achieved virtual control over 99.5 % of the non-Western world....Twenty-five years later, the western nations had lost control over all but 5 % of the non-Western population of the world.[8]

Once important Western colonial powers (England, France, Portugal, Spain) retain only a portion of their earlier importance. Their former colonies are independent states today. They don't live on dependence from their former "mother states", but are becoming partners that need to be taken more seriously (e.g. India, China, Brazil).

These countries don't want to be perceived any longer as *children*, but as real *partners*. Rather than being viewed as recipients of development aid, they want to attract economic investments. This new self-confidence is visible in many areas. For example, the "African Union" emphasizes again and again that Africa must find African solutions for African problems.

In the same way, churches in the Global South are growing in self-confidence. More and more churches are distancing themselves from a recipient mentality and developing their own potential. Likewise, a more mature and self-confident indigenous leadership is rising. This indigenous leadership often differs from Western models: it tends to be less democratic, more authoritarian, but definitely not less effective. It is a strong leadership, a leadership that is ready to bring the greatest sacrifices, and it is extremely visionary.

The terror attacks of September 11, 2001 and the ensuing American war on terror has dramatically changed the face of the world. The world has become more radical, as people fight and give their lives for their political or religious ideals.

Workers of the 11th hour are better equipped to develop their own methods and strategies to be effective. They are not limited by decades or centuries of missionary traditions which cannot easily be adapted to a world that is changing ever more rapidly. They are able to respond to changing situations by updating their strategies. They are extremely adaptable. Because they grew and matured spiritually in a dangerous and terrorized world, they are prepared for more sacrifice. They are more radical, they are ready to lay down their life for the Lamb, and in their context they view all this as *normal*.

Workers of the 11th hour realize that they live in the final hour, near the end of world and missions history. They are increasingly aware of the absolute urgency of their work.

For them, sacrifice and martyrdom are not a tragedy, but an honor. Like the New Testament workers of the 3rd hour, suffering is normative to them.

An example for this is the Chinese "Back to Jerusalem" movement. God has prepared the Chinese church through great suffering to take part in the fulfilment of the Great Commission.

One of their leaders writes:

> We knew from the beginning that there is a high price to pay for this Back to Jerusalem mission. I'm not just talking about money! I'm talking about the many Chinese who will be martyred and suffer as this vision unfolds. Many will go on one-way tickets, realizing they'll never return to China to see their loved ones again.[9]

1.3 THE CHALLENGE: THE SPIRITUAL BATTLE INTENSIFIES

Not only is the global situation becoming increasingly radical, but the spiritual powers and authorities are also becoming more radical. The closer we come to the end of world history, the more intensified the spiritual battle will become.

The end time is characterised by two opposing forces that are steadily increasing in power till the last day of world history.

Bill Hamon also notes this:

> Heaven and Hell will meet face to face in the human race. Everyone will be either divinely possessed or demon-possessed. Jesus Christ, the Commander-in-Chief of his army, will arise within his church as a mighty man of war. Jesus will be looking through the eyes of his saints at his enemy the devil.[10]

Every man is part of this battle. There will be no neutral ground and no spectators anymore.

The enemy knows that he has little time left. He intensifies the battle, mobilizing all his forces, in order to have the highest number of people under his authority.

The great war of the 21st century is not the war against terror, but the battle for souls and their eternal destiny.

> Satan's primary objective is to prevent God from being glorified by keeping lost people from being saved....Each time he succeeds he has won an *eternal victory*. Satan's secondary objective is to make human beings and human society as miserable as possible in this present life.... But this is a secondary objective because it is only a *temporal victory*.[11]

The Holy Spirit is mobilizing the church in a way never seen before in history to reach all unreached peoples. Jesus said that he would come back only when all peoples have heard the gospel:

> And this gospel of the Kingdom will be preached in the world as a testimony to all nations, *and then* end will come (Mt. 24:14; italics added by the author).

Even if the workers of the 11th hour join the harvest force rather late, and even if their employment will only last a few years, it will not be easier for them. Their service might be shorter – but more intense and demanding, as Reeve points out:

> The last won't receive a discount, a Mission without suffering. They will work in a world that increasingly defies the gospel; but they will, just as the heroes of the faith before them, enjoy the prerogative of the cross.[12]

The greatest war mankind has to face is not physical, but spiritual. Its result is not temporary, but eternal. The weapons with which the battle is fought are not visible but invisible. Advance is only possible *on knees* through fasting and prayer – and with extreme sacrifices.

In the physical war, the frontlines are getting tougher. The enemy is ever more radical, willing even to fight with his own blood (e.g. suicide bombers) to achieve his goals. In the same way, spiritual advance is only possible with great sacrifices of time, money and lives.

1.4. The Result: The Lamb of God Worshipped by All Peoples

The underlining principle of the whole history of mankind is that of worship. Since the Garden of Eden, the enemy fights to receive the worship of mankind. And since the fall of man – towards the *wrong* worship, God seeks to restore the relationship with man again and invites him to return to a life of *true* worship of the *true* God.

In the introduction to his commentary on Revelations, Pohl writes:

> Mankind prays – through all tensions that is set to rip them apart... In [Revelation] chapter 13, the confrontation climaxes. On both sides there is a focus on the essentials – there will no more be word against word – everybody will pray. „All inhabitants of the world will worship the beast – all whose names have not been written the book of life"(13:8). The "holy ones" that are seen as God's praising people will refuse to worship the beast and go into martyrdom.[13]

Every human being worships something. Either he worships the true God or he worships the beast and its associates.

But the New Testament, in particular Revelations, leaves no doubt as to who will ultimately receive the worship of mankind:

> [T]hat at the name of Jesus every knee should bow, in heaven and on earth and under the earth and every tongue confess that Jesus Christ is Lord to the glory of the father (Phil. 2:10-11).

Every knee will bow in the name of Jesus, and *every* tongue will confess Jesus as Lord. Some will do this out of joy and others will be forced to do so; but all will worship him, the true Lord.

It is the privilege of the hosts of the 11th hour to fulfill the Great Commission and, through its sacrificial work and total dedication up to the point of martyrdom, to bring forth representatives of all peoples and nations before the throne of the lamb:

> And they sang a new song: You are worthy to take the scroll and open its seals, because you were slain, and with your blood you purchased men for God from every tribe and language and people and nation (Rev. 5:9).

The entire history of missions moves towards this fantastic moment. Only on that great day will world missions have achieved its final goal, because worship has always been the ultimate goal of all missions effort, as Piper puts it so well:

Mission is not the ultimate goal of the church. Worship is. Missions exists because worship doesn't. Worship is ultimate, not missions, because God is ultimate, not man. When this age is over, and the countless millions of the redeemed fall on their faces before the throne of God, missions will be no more. It is a temporary necessity. But worship abides forever.[14]

Endnotes

1 Joseph P. Murphy, *www.worldchristiandatabase.org,* 2004.

2 Patrick Johnstone, *The Church is Bigger than You Think*, p. 110.

3 Robert Reeve, *Passion pour les nations*, p. 33.

4 Earle E. Cairns, *Christianity Through the Centuries*, pp. 134-135.

5 Ralph Winter, " Four Men, Three Eras, Two Transitions," in *Perspectives on the World Christian Movement*, ed. Ralph D. Winter and Steven C. Hawthorne, p. 259.

6 Reeve, *Passion pour les nations*, p. 38.

7 Gerhard Maier, *Matthäus-Evangelium, 2. Teil*, p. 119.

8 Winter, " The Kingdom Strikes Back," in *Perspectives on the World Christian Movement*, ed. Ralph D. Winter and Steven C. Hawthorne, p. 210

9 Brother Yun and Paul Hattaway, *The Heavenly Man*, p. 289.

10 Bill Hamon, *Apostles, Prophets and the Coming Moves of God*, p. 260.

11 C. Peter Wagner, *Warfare Prayer*, pp. 61-62.

12 Reeve, op. cit., p. 40.

13 Adolf Pohl, *Die Offenbarung des Johannes, 1. Teil*, p. 20.

14 John Piper, *Let the Nations be Glad*! p. 11.

CHAPTER 2

THE TEN MISSIOLOGICAL PRINCIPLES OF THE 11TH HOUR

2.1. WORKERS OF THE 11TH HOUR ARE PROXIMATE TO THE UNREACHED PEOPLES

The Lord of the harvest has prepared the host of the last hour in a way that it has a *worldwide presence* and is ready for action. A closer look at the spread of the church at the beginning of the 21st century reveals some interesting facts. The four countries with the highest number of evangelical Christians are spread over four continents: North America (90 million), China (76 million), Nigeria (26 million) and Brazil (21 million). The next countries on this list are in Asia (India: 18 million; Philippines: 12 million) and in Africa (Ethiopia: 12 million; Kenya: 11 million). All these countries are proximate to the last unreached people groups.

One third of all yet still unreached Muslim people groups are in Sub-Saharan Africa, but proximate to them are *116 million* evangelical Christians.[1]

This is no coincidence, but is *designed by God* for the last needed push of the church of Christ to reach *all* people groups.

The workers of the 11th hour are proximate to the unreached peoples in six ways:

2.1.1. Geographic proximity

Geographic proximity means in some cases that workers of the 11th hour and the people they want to reach live only a few kilometres away from each other.

Sometimes they are neighbors. In many capitals of the Global South, members of unreached peoples live in the immediate neighborhood of evangelical churches.

Sometimes they live in the same country. For example, in South India there are thousands of evangelical churches, while North India is one of the biggest remaining challenges for missions.

Sometimes they live in neighboring countries. In some cases, colonial powers have drawn borders, separating people groups. In one country today, there may be a strong church, while the same people in the neighboring country may still be unreached. The Hausa people of West Africa illustrates this: While in Nigeria there is a strong established, mission minded church, the same people in Niger is almost entirely unreached. In some areas, only a few kilometers separate reached and unreached villages on opposite sides of the border.

2.1.2. Cultural proximity

Cultural proximity means that though workers of the 11th hour and the people to be reached might not speak the same language, they still have similar customs and culture.

The Guera area in Chad illustrates this principle. Though there are some minor differences, the twenty or so people groups in the Guera are culturally rather homogenous. The basic cultural elements are the same all over the area. Today, the church is well established in one people group and present in at least two others. Because of their cultural proximity, they will find it much easier to reach the unreached peoples in the Guera than anyone else in the world.

2.1.3 Linguistic proximity

In many countries, sometimes even across borders, trade languages are used for communication between different peoples. In Sudan, for example, the trade language is Arabic. Many evangelical Christians of the Capital and certain areas in the South (e.g. Nuba-people) speak fluent Arabic, in some cases due to the intentional

"Arabization" by the government. Therefore, it is easier for them to reach the numerous unreached groups in the country.

In other cases, languages may not be the same, but they may have much in common. For example, they may belong to the same linguistic family, which facilitates greatly language acquisition.

2.1.4. Sociological proximity

Sociological proximity means that pioneer missionaries and those they want to reach have the same social structure. For example, most societies in the Global South are based on an extended family structure, as opposed to the nuclear family structure of the West.

In many cases, Western missionaries have used too much of an individualized approach in evangelism, whereas in the Global South the social network approach ("you *and* your house") would have been much more appropriate. For sociologically proximate workers, using this family and social network approach is natural, thereby increasing their effectiveness.

2.1.5. Economic proximity

Economic proximity means that the pioneering missionary and those to be reached have a comparable *income*.

Economic discrepancy is one of the biggest barriers to the effectiveness of Western workers:

> One of the greatest impediments to credible communication faced by Western missionaries is their relative wealth...There are numerous ways in which the relative affluence of missionaries tends to distort or otherwise hamper their effective communication of the gospel.[2]

In the eyes of a normal villager, a sermon by a rich Western missionary about a life of faith is hard to accept, because the economic discrepancy is so high. But if a rather poor missionary like himself is doing the preaching, the message will be more acceptable and have a higher impact.

Economic proximity also means that the pioneering missionary and the person that needs to be reached roughly have the same *standard of living*. So-called "Rice Christians" become Christians for financial reasons. When the missionary and the unreached have the same standard of living, people are more likely to turn to Christ because of the attraction of the person of Jesus and the gospel, and not because of the prospect of financial and economical gain.

2.1.6. Mental proximity

Mental proximity means that a worker used to a rural context is more likely to serve effectively among a rural people and a worker used to an urban context is more likely to be effective in an urban setting.

It is easier for an educated, intellectually inclined missionary to reach a more educated social class. And it is easier for a simpler, less educated missionary to reach the masses of uneducated people in the Global South.

The discrepancy between a better educated, technologically savvy Western missionary and a largely illiterate people group is usually too big to allow an effective ministry.

2.1.7. An example of missiological proximity

Missiological proximity is wherever a strong evangelical church is proximate to unreached people groups.

A good example of missiological proximity can be found in Nigeria. The church in Nigeria has a high growth rate, and according to Patrick Johnstone[3], the number of evangelical Christians today exceeds 20 million.

Many of them live in the central and northern parts of the country and are therefore fluent in Hausa, the trade language. Nigeria's northern neighbor is Niger. Things look quite different there. The number of evangelical Christians is very low, and the country is 98% Muslim.

The Nigerian church is both proximate and accessible to the unreached areas and peoples of Niger:

- Geographic proximity: They are only a few hundred, sometimes even a few dozen kilometers apart, and only one national border separates them.
- Cultural proximity: Customs in rural Nigeria and in rural Niger are virtually identical.
- Linguistic proximity: They speak the same trade language – Hausa.
- Sociological proximity: They have the same family and social structures.
- Economic proximity: They are primarily rural and agricultural.
- Mental proximity: Both have a more intellectual urban and a less educated rural population.
- Accessibility: An agreement between the two governments even allows Nigerians to travel, work and live in Niger without a visa or work permit.

The Nigerian church is an example of a church of the Global South with enormous potential to reach a neighboring country with proximate unreached people groups.

2.1.8. Conclusions regarding proximity

Proximity in most or all of the above greatly enhances missions work among unreached peoples. As a result, the workers of the Global South – the workers of the 11th hour – are qualified, one could even say predestined, to reach the unreached peoples of the Global South. They have the primary responsibility to reach them, and the greatest likelihood of an effective ministry.

This raises the question of whether workers from Latin America are really part of the hosts of the "11th hour". The answer is both yes and no. They are hosts of the 11th hour in the sense that they too have a responsibility to fulfill the great command to reach all peoples. And in light of their growing numbers and economic strength, they certainly have potential.

However, they do not meet many of the proximity criteria that will make the workers of the 11th hour most effective. In fact, Latin American workers are in the same category as North Americans and Europeans. They have similar geographic, linguistic, and cultural barriers to overcome, even though in certain cases they may be economically, sociologically and mentally proximate.

In the final analysis, in terms of the hosts of the 11th hour, the Global South cannot be defined strictly by geography. Latin-America is geographically in the Global South, but because of proximity barriers, its missionaries are effectively coming from the Global North.

Therefore, in terms of missiological proximity to unreached peoples in the Global South, North America, Europe and Latin America are from the Global North and are not ideally suited to reach them.

However, this does not in any way exempt them from carrying out their responsibilities in missions. They too are part of the hosts of the 11th hour, but their part is not the main one any more. They have neither the proximity nor the numbers to play the main part in reaching the yet unreached peoples in the Global South.

2.2. WORKERS OF THE 11TH HOUR ARE LED BY VISIONARIES OF THE RIGHT SKIN COLOR

For centuries, white was the only color that allowed a leadership role in the big missions enterprise. To have other-than-white skin meant lower rank or even submissiveness. But times have changed. Since the nations of the Global South have obtained their political independence, the self-confidence of the church has also increased. They have the growing conviction that they also can lead – and in certain contexts even much better and more effectively than any one else on the world.

The right skin colors in the leadership of the hosts of the 11th hour are not white, but black, brown and yellow; *because without local visionary leadership, the whole missions enterprise is doomed to be a failure.*

Leaders from the Global South do not normally lead by Western democratic principles, but more likely by traditional authoritative leadership principles. This might not agree with the contemporary Western image of the church, but it is not less biblical, neither is it less effective.

The hosts of the 11th hour will only move forward effectively if local leaders motivate their own people. Supervisors of the 9th hour will fail as leaders in the hosts of the 11th hour, though they may still be helpful as competent experts by giving advice.

When expatriates are in top leadership positions, it is still possible for churches of the Global South to take part in the missions endeavour, but it is impossible for them to take ownership. It will be impossible for them to take real financial ownership, although they may give minimal financial support. It will be impossible for them to send out *hosts* of workers, although they may send some.

2.3. Workers of the 11th hour are tentmakers

The contemporary model of a missionary must change. In the New Testament, Paul modelled tentmaking as a pioneering missionary lifestyle. For him, there was no discrepancy between spiritual and secular work. The whole life belonged to God, and the whole life was a sermon of the gospel.

Unfortunately, the workers of the 9th hour have modeled full support and full time "spiritual" ministry for missionaries to emerging sending structures of the Global South. Such a model is not only too expensive for most churches in the Global South, but, as we will see, in most cases it is strategically unwise.

Workers of the 11th should therefore return to Paul's tentmaker model of the New Testament.

2.3.1. Tentmakers follow the biblical model of the pioneering church planters

Paul, theologian and manufacturer of tents, was the leading pioneer missionary and church planter of the first century. He explained, modelled and defended energetically this type of ministry.

In the New Testament we find two fundamental ways to finance ministry: *tentmaking* (Paul) and *church support* (Peter). Each of them is legitimate[4] in a certain context.

Jesus called Peter to leave his fishing activity and to follow him (Luke 5:1-11). When after the death of Jesus he wanted to get back to his previous activity, Jesus renewed his calling (John 21). Years later Paul wrote about Peter that he accepted that Peter and his wife used the support model while undertaking mission journeys (1 Cor. 9:4-5). Paul knew that this was not a problem in the Jewish context (it was even expected by Jews), but that it would cause alienation in a pagan pioneer context.

As a pioneer church planter, Paul knew that he and his team would only be credible and effective as tentmakers. Therefore he insisted on using that strategy.

The examples of his church planting efforts in Thessalonica, Corinth. and Ephesus underline this strategy.

Thessalonica: On his second mission journey, Paul planted a church in Thessalonica. Reflecting on his time there years later, he wrote:

> Surely you remember, brothers, our toil and hardship; we worked night and day in order not to be a burden to anyone while we preached the gospel of God to you (1 Thess. 2:9).
> Nor did we eat anyone's food without paying for it. On the contrary, we worked day and night, labouring and toiling so that we would not be a burden to any of you. We did this, not because we do not have the right to such help, but in order to make ourselves a model for you to follow (2 Thess. 3:8-9).

These two texts show that Paul worked day and night in order to support himself. During the week, he preached the gospel while he worked. On the Sabbath, he went into the synagogues to teach the Scriptures (Acts 17:1-3).

Corinth: When Paul planted the church in Corinth, he worked as a tentmaker alongside Aquila, a Jewish businessman from Italy, who had also just arrived in Corinth (Acts 18:1-3).

Luke reports the activities of this team in Corinth:

> And because he [Paul] was a tentmaker as they were, he stayed and worked with them. Every Sabbath he reasoned in the synagogue, trying to persuade Jews and Greeks (Acts 18:3-4).

The tentmaker team worked to earn a living. Their ministry among Jews and Greeks went hand in hand with their secular work.

Years later Paul defended this strategy in his letter to the church in Corinth. In 1 Cor. 9:1-18, Paul writes about the legitimate right of servants of God to get support from the church they serve; but in the same breath he defends his strategy to not make use of this right:

> But we did not use this right. On the contrary, we put up with anything rather than hinder the gospel of Christ..... In the same way, the Lord has commanded that those who preach the gospel should receive their living from the gospel. But have I not used any of these rights... What then is my reward? Just this: that in preaching the gospel I may offer it free of charge, and so not make use of my rights in preaching it (1 Cor. 9:12b, 14-15a, 18).

We can therefore conclude that Paul used the tentmaker activity not for theological, but for strategic and contextual reasons. Later in the chapter we will discuss the reasons for this in greater detail.

Ephesus: The main ministry site of Paul's third journey was Ephesus, which was economically the most important province of the Roman Empire. Paul spent around three years there, and during these three years the whole Roman province of Minor Asia was reached by the gospel.

Even on his third journey, Paul continued his tentmaker strategy, although he did receive sporadic financial support from Philippi (2 Cor. 11:9).

Years later, on the occasion of his farewell to the elders of Ephesus, he made the following statements about his ministry among them:

> I have not coveted anyone's silver or gold or clothing. You yourselves know that these hands of mine have supplied my own needs and the needs of my companions. In everything I did, I showed you that by this kind of hard work we must help the weak, remembering the words the Lord Jesus himself said: 'It is more blessed to give than to receive' (Acts 20:33-35).

Paul applied the tentmaker model consequently, and God blessed his secular activity to such an extent that through his work he was able to not only sustain his own living but also that of his team and was even able to support "the weak".

The tentmaker model in church planting was a non-negotiable for Paul, a core principle which he did not allow to be questioned. When his apostolic ministry was in the crossfire of critics in Corinth because he worked with his hands, he once more defended vehemently this very strategy:

> Was it a sin for me to lower myself in order to elevate you by preaching the gospel of God free of charge? I robbed other churches by receiving support from them so as to serve you. And when I was with you and needed something, I was not a burden for anyone, for the brothers who came from Macedonia supplied what I needed. I have kept myself from being a burden to you in any way, and will continue to do so. As sure as the truth of Christ is in me, nobody in the regions of Achaia will stop this boasting of mine (2. Cor. 11:7-10).

Paul humbled himself through his manual labour, so that he would not be a burden to anyone in any way. He may have received occasional help from Philippi, but he didn't ask for it (Phil. 4:17) and he consistently earned his living through manual labour (2 Cor. 12:14).

The only church that ever supported Paul was Philippi. Antioch was a sending, but not a financially supporting, church. Paul writes about this in Philippians which he wrote towards the end of his two year imprisonment in Rome, roughly 63 AD,[5] which was at the very end of his missionary ministry. There he mentions that during his whole missionary career, he never received support from any other church than Philippi. Even this support seems to have been only sporadic, but his norm was to support himself through a tentmaker activity.

Here is what he wrote to the Philippians:

> As you well know, when I first brought the Gospel to you and then went on my way, leaving Macedonia, *only you Philippians* became my partners in giving and receiving. *No other church* did this. Even when I was over in Thessalonica *you sent help twice.* (Phil. 4:15-16, LB, italics added).

We see that Paul vehemently defended his use of the tentmaker model on several occasions. He worked as a tentmaker *because of a deep conviction and strategic principles,* not only when church support was not available.

Furthermore, Paul urged others to follow this example:

> We did this, not because we do not have the right to such help, but in order *to make ourselves a model for you to follow.* For even when we were with you, we gave you this rule: "If a man will not work, he shall not eat" (2. Thess. 3:9-10, italics added).

Therefore we see that tentmaking was not only the biblical model of the church planting pioneers, but also carried a strategic mandate.

2.3.2. Workers of the 11th hour have a strategic mandate to be tentmakers

Workers of the 11th hour have to make a decision to make regarding which support approach they will use. They have seen the workers of the 9th hour consistently use the church support model. However, in most cases, the church in the Global South cannot afford to send hosts of pioneer missionaries using the church support model. Should they therefore go to the churches in the Global North begging for money to send out missionaries? *No!*

Tentmakers have eight main advantages:

2.3.2.1. Tentmakers are better accepted and more credible in the eyes of the local population.

Paul vividly says that he works as a tentmaker in order to not hinder the gospel:

> If others have this right of support from you, shouldn't we have it all the more? But we did not use this right. On the contrary, we put up with anything *rather than hinder the gospel of Christ* (1. Cor. 9:12, italics added).

As mentioned above, Paul rejects financial support not for theological reasons, but for strategic reasons. He does not want to hinder the gospel; rather, he wants to be credible.

A missionary funded 100% by foreign money will be suspect to the population. His motivation will be questioned – "he only came to us because of money". In a Muslim region of sub-Saharan Africa, a missionary was told by the locals: "If we got as much money as you, we would all be Christians, too."

If the messenger is not credible, it is almost impossible to make his message credible. Before an audience accepts the *message,* it has to accept the *messenger.*

Siemens says: "He (the tentmaker) gets no financial gain out of his preaching. Instead, it costs him dearly in every way."[6]

A pioneer missionary, working as an agricultural tentmaker in a rural area, introduced by his own initiative several new planting methods. He put a great deal of effort into it and worked the largest field in the village. Accordingly, his harvest was plenty. One day the village chief told the missions leader: "If this man stays in our village, we will never be hungry again." Based on this great witness through his tentmaker work, the pioneer missionary was accepted by the local population – and on that foundation, he was able to preach the Gospel in a credible way.

2.3.2.2. Tentmakers identify themselves better with the local population.

Paul was a highly qualified theologian and was therefore able to identify himself with the Jewish *scholars* in the Synagogues and the Greek philosophers. But how was he going to reach the masses? Only by living and working like them, by placing himself on their level, by identifying with them – by following the example of Jesus in Phil. 2:5-11.

He was able to say: "We work hard with our own hands" (1. Cor. 4:12a).

He worked hard with his own hands like them, therefore he was respected by them and was able to reach the masses.

A fulltime missionary funded from the outside was told: "Pastor, you love the shade so much." In other words: "You're a lazybones, who doesn't want to work." If a missionary who lives in a rural area were the whole village does hard agricultural work doesn't work with his hands but only wants to preach, he will not be respected and therefore not be listened to.

2.3.2.3. Tentmakers proclaim the gospel through spirit-filled secular work.

Tentmakers proclaim the gospel not only in words, but also in deed. They stand in the midst of life; through an authentic Christian lifestyle they demonstrate without words that the gospel is also relevant in a "grim world," in the storms of daily life.

Through their behavior in everyday life, they preach the gospel. For instance:

- A businessman proclaims the gospel when he isn't corrupt, trades with fair prices, tells the truth and is generous.
- A judge proclaims the gospel when he does not accept bribes and always judges by the law. In an Islamic city, there was a Christian judge who was greatly respected because he never accepted bribes and was always just. After he was

transferred to a different city, the people said: "This city has never seen such a judge!"

- A teacher proclaims the gospel when he teaches with enthusiasm and dedication and always gives fair grades.
- A farmer proclaims the gospel when he labours his fields with prayer and faith in the creator.
- A nurse or doctor proclaims the gospel when he attends their patients with real love and care, and enshrouds their work with prayer for healing.

The spirit-filled performance of secular work is in itself a proclamation of the gospel without words and paves the way for verbal proclamation.

2.3.2.4. Tentmakers are at least partly financially autonomous.

The host of the 11th hour is a host from the Global South. Many of these sending structures do not have the finances to support a great number of full-time missionaries.

Tentmakers are inexpensive because they are completely, or partly, self supported. That way churches from the Global South are also in a position to send out a greater number of missionaries.

Because missionaries are financially autonomous, they are also more resistant in times of financial crisis or shortages. Unlike those who have to return home if support drops, they can stay on field, as they make their living where they minister.

2.3.2.5. Tentmakers have a natural bridge to the local population through their secular job.

In many cases, a full time missionary first has to earn the right to have access to the local population. He has to look out for opportunities to meet the people. Maybe he starts visiting people in their homes. In the eyes of the local population this is something artificial, abnormal, and unnatural.

A tentmaker, on the other hand, lives in the midst of society. Through his secular job, he has a natural connection with dozens, maybe hundreds of people, and through these natural relationships he can build bridges to extended families. In the eyes of the local population, this is quite natural and not at all suspect.

The natural bridge to the local population allows the tentmaker to pass on the gospel in a natural way.

A gardener tentmaker testified: "I find the best opportunities for spreading the gospel in the garden, under a mango tree, when we gardeners all rest together after our work." The missionary worked and sweated together with the other men of the village to feed their families and when they rested together under a mango tree he, being one of them, was able to spread the message. The garden work was the natural bridge to the other gardeners. In this way, he was able to naturally spread the gospel.

2.3.2.6. Tentmakers model a Christian lifestyle for new believers.

New believers belonging to yet unreached people groups have never seen a Christian. They cannot know how Christian ethics can manifest themselves in their society and culture.

To express it in the words of Siemens:

> Paul demonstrated Christian living because no one in the region had ever seen a Christian. He lived a holy life in the same immoral, idolatrous, cesspool society where he expected converts to live holy lives. Paul also modelled a Christian work ethic in this culture where indolence and thievery were the norm.... Paul says much in his brief letters about work, because without strong work ethic, there could not be godly converts, healthy families, independent churches – nor productive societies.[7]

Believers must be able to live without financial aid from the outside under sometimes threatening circumstances. A full time missionary cannot therefore be a role model for them.

2.3.2.7. Tentmakers model strategies for support and ministry to future church leaders.

As we will see in chapter 2.8, workers of the 11th hour work towards house church movements. Typically, house churches are lead by heads of households that work in a secular job to feed their families and welcome the church in their home.

Such small house churches or cell groups do not have the financial means to employ a full-time pastor. If the pioneering missionaries demonstrate the tentmaker model, it will seem normal to the leaders to serve their house churches as tentmakers, too.

It is only when a network of a few house churches is established, that the need for a full time shepherd will appear – but at that point the network will be financially strong enough to finance such a co-worker without help from outside.

2.3.2.8. Tentmakers can be multiplied more easily.

The hosts of the 11th hour will mainly be tentmakers, because the present structures are not serving a large host, but only a troop. If we attempt to reach all the unreached peoples in our generation by only relying on full-time and academically trained workers, we will never reach that goal.

Not every Christian is called to study theology at a seminary – but every Christian is called to spread the gospel in and through his daily life. Every mature Christian working in a secular job and living under the guidance of the Holy Spirit qualifies to minister as a tentmaker missionary among an unreached people. But not every Christian has completed a theological training that would qualify him as a full-time missionary.

2.3.3. Tentmakers are also full time missionaries.

Tentmakers minister full-time while being a full-time employee. Their tentmaker job is their God-given context, in which they permanently preach the gospel. In other words, because tentmakers are permanently with the people they want to reach, they can permanently preach – through words *and* actions.

In the meantime we should remember that only very few tentmakers work full time in a secular job. Most of them carry out a part time activity, which allows them to do church planting whilst working in the secular job (typically rather making initial contacts and low-key evangelism) and in their spare time (typically rather discipleship and edification).

Paul emphasizes the importance of *"workplace evangelism"*:

> He modelled and taught workplace evangelism because most people spent most of their time at work. Also, evangelism in the marketplace was the best way to infiltrate all of society, because it was where people of every social level rubbed shoulders. [8]

In his letters he described this strategy to the believers.

> Be wise in the way you act towards outsiders; make the most of every opportunity. Let your conversation be always full of grace, seasoned with salt, so that you may know how to answer everyone (Col. 4:5-6).

The Greek word for time that Paul uses here is "kairos" – God's time, a special opportunity. In other words: In their daily contact with non-believers, tentmakers should listen out for the Holy Spirit, so that in a God-given moment they can give a loving, polite ("full of grace") and challenging ("with a pinch of salt") word of advice.

According to this passage in Colossians, workplace evangelism consists of four fundamental elements (compare also with Eph. 6:5-8 and Col. 3:22-24):

- Personal integrity ("Be wise")
- Commitment to quality work, good use of time ("make the most of every opportunity")
- Loving, gentle relationships ("full of grace")
- Short, fitting, evangelistic comments at the right time ("with a pinch of salt")

The New Testament teaching about evangelism talks much more about lifestyle than about techniques. Our whole life is worship, and our whole life is evangelism. The tentmaker does not go out to evangelise – he himself as a person *is* evangelism and a fragrance that spreads the sweet smell of Christ.

2.3.4. Tentmakers can be extremely efficient.

The question is whether tentmakers are just as efficient as full time missionaries. Let us again listen to Paul who after a good 20 years of ministry as tentmaker writes this to the Romans:

> So from Jerusalem all the way round to Illyricum, I have fully proclaimed the gospel of Christ....But now that there is no more place for me to work in these regions... (Rom. 15:19b.23a).

In other words: Paul had completed the church planting effort in six Roman provinces – in the whole southern, Greek-speaking Mediterranean area – and had planted indigenous churches everywhere. And he did this with just a handful of missionaries from the outside and with almost no financial support.

His tentmaker job seemingly did not hinder Paul to be an extremely efficient church planter. On the contrary, his example and extraordinary commitment challenged believers and emerging leaders to follow him and preach the gospel while working as tentmakers in yet unreached areas, too.

2.3.5. How to choose the right tentmaker activity

Generally spoken, any professional activity is suitable for a tentmaker, as long as it conforms to biblical ethics.

The choice usually depends on these four factors:

- The gifts and capacities of the missionary
  Not every missionary is suited for every type of tentmaker activity – but every missionary is capable for a specific activity where he is trained and / or gifted.

- The secular education of the missionary
  Most workers of the 11th hour are heads of households that were well established in life before being commissioned. They had learned and successfully practised a profession. They will continue to work in that same profession, but from now on in an area yet unreached by the gospel.
- The realities of the new location
  Not every tentmaker activity is useful, advisable or effective in every context. In some areas, certain tentmaker activities are even impossible (e.g. in a dry, desert type of environment, farming is impossible). Therefore, before commissioning a worker, it must be carefully evaluated which tentmaker with his unique gifting and education best fits a specific area with its specific realities.
- The job opportunities in the target areas (e.g. Middle East)

Globalisation has changed the face of the world. Even strongly Islamic countries, for example in the Middle East, are looking for foreign workers. These can be highly skilled (computer engineers, scientists, doctors, professors) or unskilled (cleaners, nannies) jobs. Sending movements from the Global South can respond to these job offers by sending out their workers according to their gifting and training.

2.3.6. Examples of tentmaker activities

We conclude this chapter with a few concrete examples of tentmaker activities. However, the following list is just a sketchy outline of a few possibilities and not comprehensive. There are just as many opportunities for tentmaker activities as there are tentmakers, as each worker is an individual with a unique personality, history, experience, training and gifting.

Here are a few examples:

- farming or gardening
- fishing
- business, trade

- micro-enterprises: tailor, barber, carpenter, welder, mechanic, bricklayer, etc.
- education: adult education, teaching in private or government schools
- medical care: mobile clinic, village pharmacy, etc.
- government official transferred in a Muslim area
- Jobs in the Middle East: Highly skilled (computer engineers, scientists, doctors, professors) or unskilled (cleaner, nanny, bricklayer)

2.4. Workers of the 11th hour are sent and supported by sending structures of the Global South.

Even if the workers of the 11th hour work in partnership with those of the 9th hour, they will still be sent and supported by sending structures of the Global South.

These sending structures might not be comparable with those of the Global North. In fact they are likely to look very different, but they will be better suited for the new realities. They might be less western, but not less biblical.

There are several responsibilities for the sending structures of the Global South.

2.4.1. Selecting

The host of the 11th hour will less likely be made up of people following a "geographical call" ("I have the impression that I should serve this or this people"), but increasingly of people selected by mature leaders according to their radical commitment and tested faith.

A closer look at the concept of calling in the book of Acts shows that this method of selecting missionaries should not be considered less biblical.

The one being called	Qualifications	Calling - how?	Involvement of the called	Confirmation of the calling
Paul (9:26; 13:1-3.15-18)	Theological training Multi-lingual Enthusiasm for God Well proven in the church	First personal calling through supernatural visions Confirmation of the calling by the church through a prophetic word	Obedience towards the call of God Submission to the decision of the church leaders in Antioch	Ananias (9:15-16) Church in Antioch Prophetic words An anointed and fruitful ministry
Barnabas (11:19-26)	A proven man Full of the Holy Spirit and faith	Out of an urgent need: a leader was urgently needed; by a decision of the church elders	Is not mentioned - he submits himself to the decision of the church. Obedience	Much fruit; Joy
Timothy (16:1-3)	Good testimony, tried and tested Believing mother Receives gifts from the Holy Spirit (2 Tim 1:6)	"Paul wanted to take him along" (V 3)	Is not mentioned – he submits himself to the decision of Paul; Obedience	Through laying on of hands by the elders (1 Tim 4:14) Useful assistant to Paul
Apollos (18:24-28)	Skilled speaker Zealous, courageous, diligent Humble (26b)	"Apollos wanted to go ..." (V 27) Church supports and helps	Apollos himself takes the initiative towards his work.	Through the brothers (church) A fruitful service
Many Christians (8:1-4; 11:19-21)	Courage	Through circumstances (persecution, distress)	They are obedient and get involved in world mission; preach the word	Many conversions Fruit

Table 3: The concept of calling in the book of Acts

As table 3 illustrates, it seems that in Acts a personal calling to a specific service is only given a subordinate role. The same can be said for the commissioning model of Jesus. Jesus' call was an authoritative call, first of all towards a relationship with himself ("follow me"), that in every case lead to a specific commission into ministry later on.

Paul seemed to follow this model: those he found with radical commitment and proven faith, he called into service. Men like Timothy followed him, learned from him and thereby grew into a powerful ministry.

Many workers of the 11th hour will be sent out of a Timothy-Paul like relationship with a leader who is recognized and has an apostolic gifting. Those being sent out are expected to submit and obey their recognized leaders.

2.4.2. Training

According to Taylor, the western mission force loses every year roughly 5.1% of its members, or around 7,650 missionaries. His research regarding the reasons of this high attrition rate leads him to the following conclusion:

> Formal theological institutions that say they train missionaries often address primarily knowledge components, not character nor even skills needed to survive and thrive in cross-cultural missions.[9]

Therefore, training for the host of the 11th hour will mainly be on-the-job-training according to the faith principle in Luke 16:

> Whoever can be trusted with very little can also be trusted with much, and whoever is dishonest with very little will also be dishonest with much (Luke 16:10).

The leader first gives the potential missionary tasking to see how he develops and whether he stands the test. Faithfulness in handling these tasks and challenges is rated higher than academic and theological qualification.

Clinton points out:

> A ministry task is an assignment from God that tests a person's faithfulness...as the leader responds to them properly, God gives him tasks of greater and greater responsibility.[10]

In another paragraph Clinton writes about Barnabas:

> Barnabas' trip to Antioch in Acts 11 was an apostolic ministry task, which was definable and had closure as well as accountability to the elders in Jerusalem. It tested his apostolic gifting as well as his willingness to obey.[11]

Generally, workers of the 11th hour will be trained for ministry by a leadership using this principle of faithfulness, thus moving more and more towards an apostolic ministry.

There will always be a need for graduates from bible seminaries and missionary training schools and this is important and necessary, but in the host of the 11th hour they are in the minority.

2.4.3. Commissioning

In the commissioning of its missionaries, the sending movements of the 11th hour follow the model described in Acts 13:

> While they were worshipping the Lord and fasting, the Holy Spirit said, "Set apart for me Barnabas and Saul for the work to which I have called them." So after they had fasted and prayed, they, placed their hands on them and sent them off (Acts 13:2-3).

The workers of the 11th hour will first and foremost be sent out by the Holy Spirit that speaks through the church. The church of the Global South under fasting and prayer sends out their best and highly proven people to pioneering missionary church planting work.

Only people that have proven themselves over years of fruitful service and been loyal to the church are sent. They comply with the qualifications required for elders, just as Paul writes in Acts (see diagram 4 below). Normally they will be younger or older couples, and in many cases families.

As explained above (Chapter 2.3), missionaries are sent out as tentmakers. In most cases they serve in the profession they had been trained in and according to their spiritual gifting. In fact, they live just as before, but now in a different area, unreached by the gospel.

2.4.4. Financing

We will look at different financing models in much greater detail in chapter three. It is enough for now to mention that workers of the 11th hour do not hope for financial support from their sending church. They might receive initial help or small regular support over a short period of time, according to the models presented in chapter three; but in general they are autonomous due to their tentmaker jobs.

As in the case of Paul, sporadic gifts in times of need are possible but an exception.

2.4.5. Coaching and Member Care

The sending movement makes sure that the pioneering missionary is on task and strives towards his aim of planting indigenous church planting movements.

As O'Donnell correctly states:

> Cultures differ significantly in their ways to confront, encourage, resolve conflicts, express feelings, and show affection. The way problems are identified and the type of help that is seen to be appropriate also vary greatly.[12]

As their way of coaching and counselling is very different from Western methods, it is much more effective if the sending structure of the Global South assumes this responsibility.

> The notion that formal education rather than broad experience qualifies one to be a counsellor seems to be a largely Western notion. "Lay people," especially heads of nuclear and extended families, play a much larger helping and guiding role in non-Western churches as compared to Western cultures.... In the Philippines, for example, even the civil code says that grandparents shall be consulted by all members of the family on all important questions.[13]

Where humans work together, sooner or later there will be conflicts. These are dealt with very differently in non-Western cultures. Where coaching and member care are exercised by leaders of the Global South, non-western approaches to peacemaking include strategies such as mediation and mediators, the one-down position and vulnerability, storytelling and proverbs, inaction, misdirection, silence and indefinite persons.[14] This will lead to less misunderstandings and a more effective conflict management.

2.4.6. Assuming the final responsibility

Workers of the Global South do not set off in the name of their western partner, but in that of the church, denomination, or missions movement of the Global South. These missionaries "belong" to them. Only in this way can true indigenous ownership of the missionary enterprise can be guaranteed.

Even if some of the workers of the 11th hour are sent out with western partners through partnership models, the final responsibility still lies completely with the sending structure of the Global South, whether in financial crisis, political unrest, spiritual crisis, emotional problems or physical sickness.

No Western partner will ever be able to lead workers of the Global South as effectively as an indigenous leader.

2.5. Workers of the 11th hour rate personal maturity higher than academic training

Only very few workers of the 11th hour are in possession of diplomas or academic titles. Among them exist only a minority who have spent years in a classroom – but most of them have spent years in the midst of life and have thereby grown into mature personalities.

The host of the 11th hour is made up of men and women that are qualified for ministry because of their maturity, rather than because of their diplomas. They are men and women that have received great authority through the anointing of the Holy Spirit, not through positions and titles conferred by men.

They rate the qualifications necessary for deacons of higher importance than academic qualifications:

> Brethren, look ye out among you seven men of honest report, full of the Holy Ghost and wisdom, whom we may appoint over this business (Acts 6:3, KJV).

A mature personality will have these three features: personal integrity (honest report; good testimony), fullness of the Holy Spirit, and discernment (full of wisdom). This human and spiritual maturity will help them to minister effectively, as Luke reports about Stephen, one of the seven chosen deacons: "Now Stephen, a man full of God's grace and power, did great wonders and miraculous signs among the people" (Acts 6:8).

Mature personalities prove their competence for an apostolic ministry through spiritual, moral-emotional and social competence. They manage their families well and have ministry skills, too. They thereby follow the requirements of Paul for church leaders. However, of these five areas of New Testament elder qualifications, the first four are more important than the area of ministry skills, as important as those might be.

The following table summarizes the qualifications that Paul requires for church leaders (compare: 1 Tim. 3:1-7; Tit. 1:5-9; 1 Pet. 5:1-4).

The pioneer missionary cannot be effective if he is unable to build and maintain good relationships. Just as Daryl Platt correctly states, "Personal relationships form the heart of cross-cultural ministry."[15]

Therefore, a special emphasis must be put on moral, emotional and social competence.

2.6. WORKERS OF THE 11TH HOUR WORK IN PARTNERSHIP WITH WORKERS OF THE 9TH HOUR

No generation is ever exempt from the Great Commission. All churches of all times on all continents are called to reach all nations of their generation. From that perspective, it is incorrect to say that

Spiritual competence	**Moral & Emotional competence**	**Managing the family well**	**Social competence**	**Ministerial competence**
Holy and disciplined (is striving for sanctification) Keeps the teachings of the Word of God (is rooted in the word of God and loves it wholeheartedly) Does not lord over the flock Not a new convert Serves freely and with dedication, for God, without any compulsion; is eager to serve Has a clear conscience	Sober Not given to drunkenness Temperate Decent Not a lover of money Not pursuing dishonest gain Under authority Self-controlled Loves the good Honourable / Respectable Not deceitful	Husband of one wife (not polygamous; is faithful to his wife) Manages his household well Children are respectful and obedient Has children who follow the Lord and do not have an excessive lifestyle	Has a good reputation with outsiders so that he will not fall into disgrace and into the devil's trap Is above reproach / blameless Lifestyle of integrity Not violent Mild Not quick tempered Righteous Hospitable	Able to teach Able to encourage others by sound teaching Able to refute those who oppose sound doctrine Able to shepherd God's flock

Table 4: Signs of a mature personality that qualify for ministry

western churches have no role to play anymore and should leave the Great Commission to the churches of the Global South.

In other words, even if the host of the 11th hour comes mainly from the Global South, the Western church still has an important role to play in fulfilling the Great Commission.

The two most important roles of the western church in the 21st century can be summed up in two words: pioneering mission work and partnership.

Pioneering mission work through workers of the 9th hour is important in places where no workers of the 11th hour are in geographical, cultural, linguistic, sociological, economical, and mental proximity or in areas where it is very difficult for them to get to.

Partnerships are needed where workers of the 9th hour are invited and welcome. This will happen in contexts where they are able to make a real contribution towards maximizing the effectiveness of the mission work.

Mature churches of the Global South realize that they are more effective through partnerships. These partnerships should not be established just "for the sake of the partnership," but to use potential synergies strategically.

Fundamental for any real partnership is the complementary contribution of every partner. Dependence on the West must be avoided at all costs. The Western partner should only contribute what the partner of the Global South is not able to do *and should always encourage him to take on his own responsibilities.*

In these partnerships workers of the 9th hour can have the following functions:

2.6.1. To catalyze

A catalyst in chemical terms is:

> A substance that increases the rate of a chemical reaction without being consumed in the reaction. A substance that lowers the activation energy for a chemical reaction by providing an alternate pathway for the reaction."[16]

Catalysts make possible or speed up sending movements from the Global South. As catalysts, workers of the 9th hour develop solid relationships with those in their region that are growing in passion to love and serve unreached people groups.

The goal is to see these relationships blossom into sending movements that will put many apostolically-called and well-prepared workers on the field and keep them there long enough to establish indigenous communities.

Catalysts seek to serve these emerging African and Asian sending movements by encouraging *their* initiatives, *their* patterns of engagement, *their* development of models for ministry and *their* sending structures.

Catalysts don't recruit co-worker for their own mission agencies - they rather join the sending movements of the Global South and ideally work in *their* name and under *their* leadership.

The following graph[17] summarizes the partnership responsibilities which workers of the 9th hour have as catalysts:

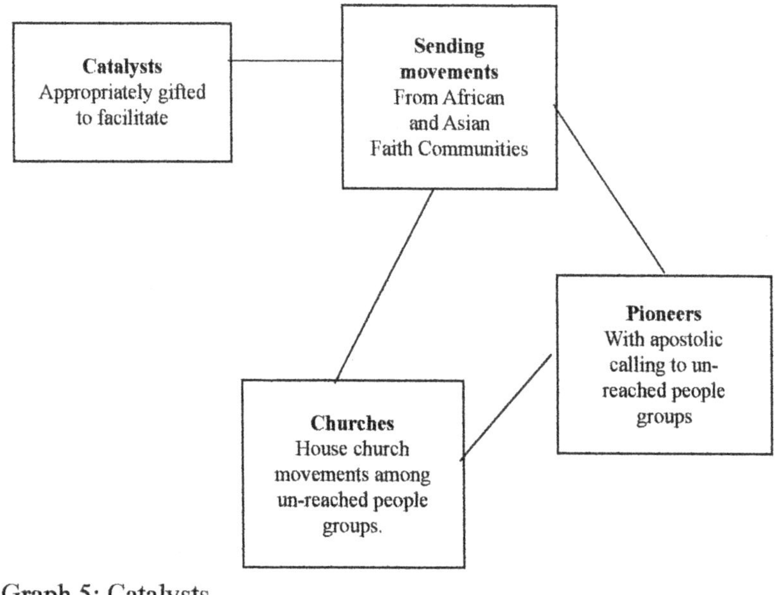

Graph 5: Catalysts

2.6.2. To model

In certain areas, workers of the 11th hour are far ahead of the workers of the 9th hour. These are often areas such as boldness in ministry, self denial, willingness to suffer and to die or, as in the case of the Chinese house church movement, multipliable and persecution-resistant church structures. In other areas, workers of the 9th hour are expected to be models. These can be areas such as contextualization, language acquisition techniques or teamwork.

But modelling should never be more than exactly that, following the motto "model – assist – observe – go." If the modelling leads to paternalism, it has failed. By any means, modelling should lead to an autonomous indigenous sending movement.

2.6.3. To train

Workers of the 9th hour have 200 years of missionary experience. It is part of their responsibility to be good stewards by passing these experiences on to new workers. If they don't do so, they waste valuable resources and condemn the emerging mission movements of the Global South to repeat the same mistakes.

Some Christians in the West assume that indigenous workers are in any case more effective than western workers. This is only half true: local workers are not by any means better than foreigners – but *well trained* local workers are in most cases more effective.

The training we talk about should not be equalled with academic-theological education. It rather means short, specific, need- and practise-oriented training. It usually takes the form of short seminars and conferences. For instance, an expert on a specific topic is invited at an interdenominational meeting for all workers of a certain region for empowerment in a specific ministry area. This training happens on-site, in a simple environment and with locally available means.

The importance of on-site training through short seminars is highlighted in the development literature, too. Research has shown that only 10% of graduates of a several years long, distant training facility actually end up doing developing work. The percentage of those who were supported during that time was even lower. In contrast, most of the graduates of locally organized, shorter and smaller, practice orientated training courses were self-sufficient and active in development work.[18]

2.6.4. To finance in partnership

The balance between the two extremes – "paternalism" (we will do *everything* for you) and unkindness (do it yourself, we will do *nothing* for you) – must be maintained at all costs. There are indeed ways to partner that hold responsibilities for both parties, do not hinder multiplication, maintain the dignity of the Global South, and in the long-term lead to autonomous sending movements.

In this context, it is crucial that Western money is only used *as scarcely as possible* and that *dependency is avoided by any means.* Development strategists have come to the same conclusion as the following quote shows:

> In summary, neither giving things to people nor doing things for people will be of much long-term benefit, and both may have serious negative side effects. Development is basically a process whereby people learn to participate constructively in the solving of their own problems. The driving force behind this participation is enthusiasm; the direction in which the people must move is toward gradually increasing participation; and the goal is that the program itself gradually be lost in, and replaced by, a totally participatory movement of the people, by the people, and eminently for the people.[19]

A temporary shortcut of these principles (i.e. 100 % funding with Western money of workers from the Global South) might lead to the sending of a few workers and bring about fast short term results, but it will prevent sending *movements* and in the long term have destructive consequences – for it chokes the initiative of the church in the Global South, does not allow it to take on its own responsibility, and ultimately degrades it.

This is also the experience of George Verwer who says:

> A great problem created by the emphasis being put on the financial support of nationals by churches in the West, rather than the sending of missionaries, is that of dependency....When I first went to Mexico I was still a college student, so the only thing I could do was to get Mexicans mobilised while I supplied the finance, through prayer, for the work they were doing. The first national I worked with left the work 15 or so years later because he found it so difficult to live off American money. He was a Mexican and he didn't want to do that any more.[20]

In chapter 3 we will look in greater detail at eleven models for financing in partnership.

2.6.5. To coach

Workers of the 9th hour assist the sending movement of the Global South by coaching and mentoring its *leaders*.

Many of these mentors will not necessarily live among an unreached people. They will rather inspire, encourage and coach from the outside, from the Global North. This will be the new category, the new role of the so-called "non-residential missionaries". They may not always be on-site, but this does not mean that they will be less effective. However, most of these non-residential missionaries will only be heard and effective in the measure they are themselves spiritually mature and anointed, have long-term missions experience and minister presently in a fruitful work.

2.7. WORKERS OF THE 11TH HOUR USE SUSTAINABLE AND MULTIPLIABLE STRATEGIES

Though workers of the 11th hour do partner with workers of the 9th hour, they are not financially and materially dependent on them. They may accept initial or sporadic, one-time help thankfully and humbly.

Nevertheless, they grow and multiply through *locally available* personnel, material and financial resources.

2.7.1. Locally available personnel resources

Sustainability and multiplication are only possible when personnel resources are available locally.

Training through western partners therefore has to aim at the training of trainers that can pass on what they have learned.

The Timothy Principle of Paul must be followed:

> And the things you have heard me say in the presence of many witnesses entrust to reliable men who will also be qualified to teach others (2 Tim. 2:2).

In view of multiplication, the aim of any activity of western partners should be to locally train personnel resources. There is a mission school in Africa that, since its beginnings in the early 1990s, has always invited the same western trainer for the same teaching sessions. Should it not be possible within ten years to train an African partner to do the same teaching?

2.7.2. Locally available material resources

Sustainability and multiplication are only possible when material resources are locally available.

Western partners should therefore at all cost avoid strategies that will later be impossible to be sustained and multiplied locally.

Western missionaries are often dependent on western technology that is not available locally or not affordable for most workers of the Global South. If evangelism and church life is dependent on western technology, multiplication or even small growth is choked.

The host of the 11th hour renounces western technology and works with resources that are locally available and culturally and socially suitable.

2.7.3. Locally available financial resources

Sustainability and multiplication are only possible when financial resources are available locally. Where finances are not generated locally, the whole operation is doomed for failure sooner or later.

It is an error to believe that finances are not available locally. And it is an even worse error to take the shortcut of western financial support, rather than to take the painful, rocky road of local funding.

If missionary projects cannot be funded locally, it might be better to wait until the necessary means are available.

Since the beginning of the nineties a large evangelism campaign has taken place every year in Chad, called "Chad for Christ." Every year all the churches are mobilized and every year finances are too tight to finance the one week event. The leaders finally addressed the problem by using a local way of financing: "Operation Koro."The churches might think that they do not have any financial means, cash or money on bank accounts. But they all have something that they can contribute. A "Koro" is a set measure of a bowl (e.g. sugar, tea, wheat). Every believer was urged to give one "Koro" of what they had towards the campaign. By doing so a good part of the campaign could be financed locally.

It is a sign of paternalism if a church of the Global South is prevented the right to give, because there is enough or too much Western funding. It is a right and a duty for *every* believer on *every* continent at *any* time to financially support the spread of the Kingdom.

The one who gives is more blessed than the one who receives. Giving is a blessing. Whoever does not allow the emerging movements of the Global South to participate in the fulfilment of the Great Commission through contributing financially is robbing them of a spiritual blessing!

2.8. Workers of the 11th hour are radically contextual and work towards insider movements

In the history of missions, contextualization has only recently been a major topic. Only after the era of colonialism did the topic become an important field for study and research for missiologists and missionaries. Most books on contextualization were written in the last two decades.

Lingenfelter gives the following definition for contextualization:

> The idea of contextualization is to frame the gospel message in language and communication forms appropriate and meaningful to the local culture, and to focus the message upon crucial issues in the lives of the people.[21]

2.8.1. Biblical examples and mandates for contextualization

Jesus himself lived radically contextual. He could have stayed in heaven and preached the love of God from there. But he who

> being in very nature God, did not consider equality with God something to be grasped, but made himself nothing, taking the very nature of a servant, being made in human likeness, and being found in appearance as a man (Phil. 2:6-8a).

In his appearance Jesus did not differ from his contemporaries. He lived just like a normal Palestinian Jew in the first century. He talked, ate, drank, dressed, worked, and behaved culturally just like every one else.

But in his inner being he differed fundamentally from his contemporaries. He was the Son of God, without shortcoming, without sin, in permanent community and harmony with the father. He shared his whole life with other humans, but without taking part in their sin, without hypocrisy and in absolute holiness.

His contextualization was so perfect that even his enemies were not able to distinguish him from others: a traitor's kiss by one of his closest companions was needed to arrest him (Luke 22:47-48).

Paul lived radically contextual. Even though he was free and did belong to no man, he took on different roles with the one purpose to overcome all cultural barriers and win the highest possible number of people from different cultural backgrounds for the gospel.

In the well-known passage of 1 Cor. 9:19-23, Paul describes his position and the different contextual roles that he took on to win people (italics added):

> Though I am free and belong to no man, I make myself a slave to everyone, *to win* as many as possible. To the Jews I became like a Jew, *to win* the Jews. To those under the law I became like one under the law (though I myself am not under the law), so as *to win* those under the law. To those not having the law I became like one not having the law (though I am not free from God's law, but am under Christ's law), so as *to win* those not having the law. To the weak I became weak, *to win* the weak. I have become *all things to all men* so that *by all possible means* I might save some. *I do all this* for the sake of the gospel, that I may share in its blessings (1 Cor. 9:19-23).

Paul underlines that a contextual lifestyle is never an end in itself. The key word in this passage is "to win" (5x). The ultimate purpose of contextualization is to win men. To become *all* things to *all* men so that by *all* means some might be saved.

In addition to these biblical models, we also have *biblical mandates* for a contextual approach. Jesus tells us, 'As the Father has sent me, I am sending you' (e.g. contextual, see John 20:21); Paul urges us to have the same attitude as Christ (Phil. 2:5) and to follow his example as he follows Christ's (1 Cor. 11:1); Peter reminds us that we are called "so that you should follow in his steps" (1 Pet. 2:21).

After quoting Peter, Lingenfelter correctly concludes:

> If Jesus really did give an example, then that means to me that I have to put in just as much energy, to become Yapese, just as he did

> to become a Jew. With the Missions order Jesus sent us into all the world, and as his messengers we have to follow in his steps. That means "to become people" of the cultures we are sent to.[22]

In the following four sections, we will investigate the areas in which a contextual approach must express itself.

2.8.2. The Contextual Messenger

Firstly, a contextual approach expresses itself through the messenger as a person. If he really wants to work towards an insider movement, he must first become an insider himself. Before the unreached population accepts the message, it must accept the messenger.

A close study of all aspects of the messenger's life that need to be contextual would go beyond the scope of this work. We lack the time to study the traditional areas of contextualization (language, time orientation, nutrition, lifestyle, family life etc.). We prefer to just refer to the very relevant work of Lingenfelter / Mayer (The 12 basic cultural orientations).[23]

However, two important factors need to be pointed out here.

2.8.2.1. The Economical Factor

At the *economical level,* it is virtually impossible for the western missionary to truly live contextual. The many material goods that seem absolutely necessary for the ministry and indispensable for "normal" life create a distance to the local population that makes contextualization impossible.

The workers of the Global South on the other hand are economically proximate to the unreached people (see chapter 2.1.). It is considerably easier for them to identify with the local population, because they are able to live the same lifestyle and for economical reasons may even be compelled to do so.

2.8.2.2. The Power Factor

The Western missionary is in most cases oriented towards the intellect. To him being a missionary means to *verbally* spread the biblical message. His mission is completed when his counterpart *intellectually* understands his message.

However, most of the yet unreached people groups are much more oriented towards experience. For them, the fulfilment of physical and emotional needs is much more important than the acquisition of knowledge. In such a context, demonstrating power is therefore much more important than demonstrating knowledge.

The religious teacher is expected to be just as competent at the level of power as at the level of knowledge. The ability to diagnose, treat, and heal is a substantial part of religious teaching. Or to express it with the words of Lothar Käser,

> all medical terms have religious roots. Therefore the healer is also always the expert in the area of religion and all his treatment has a fundamentally religious character.[24]

In cultures with folk Islamic practices, all healing methods are inseparably interwoven with religion. If the religious teacher really wants to be perceived as an authority, he needs to be competent in the areas of treating and healing illnesses.

Though these concepts are foreign to most Western missionaries, they are not at all unusual for the workers of the Global South. They consider normative for themselves and their ministries what Paul wrote to the Corinthians:

> My message and my preaching were not with wise and persuasive words, but with a demonstration of the Spirit's power, so that your faith might not rest on men's wisdom, but on God's power (1 Cor. 2:4-5).

After quoting this verse, Sobhi Malek explained: "The Greek word translated here as 'demonstration' literally means proof something that is forceful enough to bring conviction."[25]

For workers of the Global South, verbal declarations and demonstrations of God's power go hand in hand thus following the proclamation model of the first apostles who fervently prayed:

> Now Lord, consider their threats and enable your servants to speak your word *(verbal proclamation)* with great boldness. Stretch out your hand to heal and perform miraculous signs and wonders *(demonstration of God's power)* through the name of your holy servant Jesus (Acts 4:29-30; italics added).

After his analysis of Philips' ministry in Samaria (Acts 8:5-24), Love comes to the correct conclusion that he not only spoke

> ... of *reconciliation* with God, but also *release* from Satan, emphasizing *forgiveness* through Christ as well as *freedom* from Satan.[26]

2.8.3. The contextual Message and its contextual proclamation

2.8.3.1. The contextual Message

It is not only the life of the messenger that must be contextual. The proclamation must be contextual, too. This means not only proclaiming the Good News, but proclaiming it in a way that is understood as good news!

Obviously the gospel in itself is unchangeable. But a study of its proclamation in the Bible shows that the message does adapt to its particular audience:

Jesus himself proclaimed a contextual message according to the needs of his audience: for example, Nathaniel (John. 1 –a word of knowledge), Nicodemus (John 3 –a theological debate), and the Samaritan woman (John 4 – where and how God is to be worshiped).

Paul did the same, as a study of the book of Acts shows. He adapted the message to the Jews (Acts 13 – using arguments from the Old Testament), to the pagans (Acts 14 – no reference to the Old Testament, but signs and wonders), and to the Greeks (Acts 17 – reference not to the Old Testament, but to Greek philosophers).

An effective message has to be a contextual message. Only so can it be truly relevant and touch the hearts at their deepest level. The messenger therefore needs to not only know the word of God, but also the heart of the people, so that he can proclaim a message that addresses the needs of those who listen. An effective message begins at the level of a felt need of the audience.

According to Warren, this was the fundamental evangelistic strategy of Jesus:

> People gathered around Jesus, because he fulfilled their needs – physical, emotional, spiritual, in relationships and financial..... Jesus often confronted need, to establish a "Landing place for Evangelisation" in the life of a person..... It is not important *why* people came to Christ, but *that* they did.[27]

2.8.3.2. The contextual proclamation of the Message

Hesselgrave stresses that it is not only the content of the message that should be addressed, but also *the channel of communication:*

> For better or worse, the very media by which the missionary conveys the Christian message will carry their own "messages" and promote their own changes. Only as the missionary understands this fact will he be able partially to control this extra-Christian change process and assist his respondents as they experience it.[28]

The channel which the missionary uses for the communication of the gospel is in itself a message. Therefore the mediums used should be as contextual as possible.

Western missionaries tend to use expensive and highly sophisticated equipment to spread the gospel. They transfer methods from their culture and use them without adaptation in a completely different context. What they thereby unconsciously proclaim is not only the gospel, but also the supremacy of western technology.

Workers of the 11th hour are often forced, mostly out of economical reasons, to use contextual tools. They observe how religious teachers in their host country convey their teachings and then select their own methods accordingly. This may mean to preach with a simple megaphone at a market place, to teach small groups in a house, to read scriptures publicly at a street corner, or to play a message using a manual tape recorder.

An example of this is supplied by Livingstone. He shows how a converted Arab Muslim in Cairo spread the message in a contextual way in a tea house; accompanied with the local favorite drink (tea), the word of God is treated with respect (first it is kissed, the forehead touched with it and then opened with dignity), then read in Muslim intonation. The Word is then taught in the heart language.[29]

Contextual methods lead towards an insider movement, because they are easily reproduced: all needed equipment is available locally and within financial reach.

2.8.4. Contextual Church Planting

2.8.4.1. Contextual church planting aims at church planting movements, not at individual churches.

Only church planting *movements* can penetrate whole nations with the gospel.

A church planting movement is:

> ...a rapid and exponential increase of indigenous churches planting churches within a given people group or population segment.[30]

The pioneering missionaries need to develop specific strategies that aim at a church planting movement, because they will usually only achieve what they expect.

> If the church planting team expects to witness to a few people that is what will happen. If they expect to see a few being faithful to the Lord that is likely what they will realize. If, from the beginning, the team and the sponsoring churches envision a congregation with its own elders living openly in faith and obedience to the living Lord Jesus Christ, they are much more likely to see such a congregation become a reality.[31]

If a church planting movement is the ultimate goal of their ministry, the missionaries must work towards it from the very first day. After numerous studies on church planting movements, Garrison concludes that they have all the following common factors: prayer, sowing the gospel abundantly, local lay leadership, cell or house churches, rapid reproduction, etc.[32] These factors have to be included in the church planting strategy right from the start.

The members of a church need to understand that its aim is growth, multiplication and mission:

> When a church is planted, it has to be a missionary church from the start. Every church needs to be aware that it doesn't only live to receive the blessing of good, but to share it.[33]

2.8.4.2. Contextual Church Planting practices Oikos-Evangelism

Many Western missionaries are well trained in the area of personal evangelism, because western societies view the individual so highly.

> Too often with our Protestant, nineteenth-century individualism, we have torn men and women one by one out of the family, village, or clan with the result that they have been permanently deracinated and maladjusted... Experience shows that it is much better if an entire natural group – a family village, caste or tribe – can come rapidly over into the faith. That gives reinforcement to the individual Christian and makes easier the Christianization of the entire life of the community.[34]

Many non-Western cultures place a higher value on the nuclear and extended family rather than on the individual. Evangelism should therefore aim at winning whole families and social networks. This "Oikos Strategy" (oikos: Greek for home, family, household[35]) was already successfully used by Jesus and the first apostles:

> Jesus constantly did His work by invading *oikos* groups. He knew there was no other way to share the gospel except to penetrate these small clusters of people.... The penetration of *oikoses* is the pattern for ministry in the first century. Conversions are frequently recorded

> as sweeping an entire *oikos* into the Kingdom. In Acts 16, both Lydia and the jailer are converted along with the members of their *oikos*.[36]

Just as the Holy Spirit led Peter to Cornelius, the church planter will be led to men of peace and women of honour that will then be able to penetrate their whole social networks.

> Jesus in Luke 10:1-9 instructs the 70 as they go into towns to look for a "man of peace". This man is already prepared to receive the good news of God's Kingdom. He has a good reputation and has good relationships with many others in the community. This man's home becomes the center of activity for the "evangelist", from which the gospel penetrates the whole community.
> This became the strategy by which the early apostles penetrated the world with the good news of Jesus Christ.[37]

Evangelism aims at heads of households. To win the head of a family also means to win a potential leader, a potential new church and a potential new meeting place. It does not matter where they would meet, in a hanger, under a tree, in a villa or in a small mud hut – a new location is won, and multiplication is pre-programmed.

Considering the people group as a whole, such men of peace are strategic for a multiplying insider movement:

> Instead of trying to reach every individual in our target group ourselves, outsiders can establish a cross-cultural beachhead by ministering in-depth to some. We then trust the Holy Spirit to use the resulting believers, who as cultural insiders can help their own people more effectively than we ever could.[38]

"Oikos" does not only mean family, but also tribe or race. Oikos evangelism does not only aim at families, but at the winning of homogeneous entities. McGavran calls this a people movement that results from

> .... the joint decision of a number of individuals – whether five or 500 – all from the same people which enables them to become Christians without social dislocation while remaining in full contact with their non-Christian relatives, thus enabling other groups of that

> people across the years after suitable instruction to come to similar decisions and form Christian churches made up exclusively of members of that people.[39]

Workers of the 11th hour are more likely to understand the importance of "Oikos Evangelism" as a strategy, because in most cases they themselves come from an oikos-oriented background.

2.8.4.3. Demonstrations of power are an integral part of the Contextual Church Planting Process

What has already been mentioned above as power demonstrations must be repeated here: Workers of the 11th hour work with little or no advanced technology, therefore much more with New Testament authority.

They expect that God proves his word through signs and wonders just as in the book of Acts, and this especially in the context of church planting.

Love quotes a worker in Central Asia that through experience came to believe that

> ...power encounter must be part of the church-planting process.[40]

And Wimber recognizes:

> It seems as though God takes delight to heal difficult cases in the context of evangelism. These healings confirm the proclamation of the gospel and are demonstrations of the power of God.[41]

Especially in a pioneer context it seems as though God takes delight in confirming the coming of his Kingdom through signs and wonders.

2.8.5. The Contextual Church

Contextual church planting must lead to contextual churches. In the following sections we will investigate some of the fundamental characteristics of a contextual church:

2.8.5.1. House Churches as the Normal and Normative Church Structure

Church buildings are neither a structure that is easily multiplied (too expensive) nor able to withstand persecution (too visible, in certain contexts too provocative).

Therefore the churches planted by the host of the 11th hour follow the example of Jesus (who often taught *in homes*– Luke 10:38-39; 7:36-50; John 13:17; John 3) and the first Christians during the time of Acts (italics added):

- Greet.... the church *in their home*! (Rom. 16:3.5)
- They greet you ... Aquila and Priscilla and the church *in their home* (1 Cor. 16:19)
- Greet... Nympha and the church *in their home*! (Col. 4:15)
- *From house to house,* they never stopped teaching and proclaiming the good news. (Acts 5:42)
- Practice *hospitality!* (Rom. 12:13b).

We should not forget that in the first decades, even in the first centuries, there were no church buildings:

> We should remember that during the time of the first Christians, the church did not own a specific building. The Christians met in their homes. The first churches were only built about 200 years after the era of Paul.... This means that during the early days of the church there existed hundreds and hundreds of small gatherings, lead by elders.[42]

In the 11th as well as in the 3rd hour, the emphasis is much less on denominations as on city-churches (the church of....): the city-wide church of Christ that meets in countless homes.

> Church planting then meant to proclaim the gospel in word and deed, and to gather those who believed into fellowship groups, meeting in homes. Those in a given city who were called followers of Jesus Christ were the church in that particular city.[43]

The house church structure in conjunction with a "city church" can, as the example of China impressively shows, survive even in the most hostile context. It is persecution resistant and therefore by all means able to survive and even multiply in a world that is hostile towards the gospel.

2.8.5.2. Church is perceived as organism, not as organization – the Church life is relationship, not program oriented.

Because contextual churches meet in homes, the life of the church focuses on families. Rigid programs are replaced by a loose, informal family atmosphere.

A family is not an organization whose members formally meet weekly. A family is much more an organism whose members are interdependent.

An analysis of the early church shows that common meals were one of the main purposes of their meetings (Acts 2:47; 1 Cor. 11:33). Common meals were a demonstration of their unity and fellowship as the family of God.

> In some nations a treaty is signed or peace is declared with a meal. When people from radically different cultures or social classes eat together, they proclaim a prophetic message: We are one family, look, we even eat together![44]

A joint meal between the members of a house church is the mortar that holds the relationships together; the place where informal counselling, teaching, and encouragement take place. But it is also an opportunity to invite friends and demonstrate the gospel message of love by being a hospitable Christian family.

In this intimate atmosphere, evangelism is very effective:

> It is easier to invite friends or neighbours to a small group meeting where everyone is noticed than to an impersonal church service... What happens there among the members of the home church, the quality of their lives, their listening, their sharing, their teaching and their prayers are in themselves evangelistic – even without big speeches and intellectual appeal.[45]

2.8.5.3. Leadership is provided by bi-vocational elders (heads of households), not full time pastors

As in the Book of Acts, house churches are lead by elders, heads of households that usually work as tentmakers.

Garrison, who studied church planting movements, came to the conclusion that lay people in leadership are a key to fast growth:

> Church Planting Movements are driven by lay leaders. These lay leaders are typically bi-vocational and come from the general profile of the people group being reached. As the movement unfolds, paid clergy often emerge. However, the majority – and growth edge of the movement – continue to be led by lay or bi-vocational leaders.[46]

These church leaders meet the biblical qualifications for elders (table 4). They are not expected to have a formal academic theological training, first and foremost they are expected to have a mature and spiritual personality; the gift of teaching; a flawless life style and testimony within the inner circle of the community (family, house church) as well as in the wider circle (tentmaker activity, society); the gift to shepherd a fellowship.

These elders will be trained on-site using Bible courses adapted to their context to avoid alienating them from their family, working and social environment.

To ensure multiplication at all times, such house church leaders are not given financial support from the outside. They support themselves through tentmaker activities.

2.8.5.4. Corinthian gatherings: everyone is involved

Paul encourages all believers in Corinth to contribute to the church meetings according to their gifting:

> What then shall we say, brothers? When you come together, *everyone* has a hymn, or a word of instruction, a revelation, a tongue or an interpretation. All of these must be done for the strengthening of the church (1 Cor. 14:6, italics added).

Simson describes such an informal house church meeting:

> It would be typical for such a teaching time during the meeting of an extend family to give a short introduction, a picture, a parable, some examples that get the conversation going – often interrupted by sounds of approval or by others asking for more tea or sweets. Usually, this leads to a time of questions and answers. An interactive and dynamic teaching method as everyone is able to participate and obtain the explanations he or she is seeking.[47]

2.8.5.5. The form of the church is contextual

The form of the church will also adapt to the specific context.

The principles and practices of church life must of course have their roots in the New Testament. Nevertheless, at the level of cultural adaptation, the church planter should be just as flexible as the New Testament: not less, not more. In other words, where the New Testament is absolute he should hold to the dogma. Where it is not specific, he should encourage a contextual approach within the framework of the New Testament.

Here are some possible examples, especially within an Islamic context, without claiming to be exhaustive.

- Naming of Believers

Just the word "Christian" calls about negative emotions for many Muslims. For many of them Christianity is connected with crusades, materialism, moral decay in the West or with American world conquest. To call themselves "Christians" would mean to betray their own people.

The newly established church might therefore search for other, though not less biblical ways, to avoid unnecessary barriers: possible naming of believers could be "messianic Muslims", "followers of the Messiah" or just "Believers".

➢ Prayer forms

The western church has developed prayer forms that might not defy scriptural teachings, but are not found within them neither. Examples for this are praying with closed eyes or sitting on a chair. For a converted Muslim this can be very alienating, and he will therefore look for other, more contextual prayer forms.

Phil Parshall says:

> With certain key alterations or substitutions, the Muslim convert can continue in the familiar pattern of prayer which is valued both by him and by his Islamic society....In the Old Testament lifting up of the hands toward heaven accompanied kneeling or standing (cf. Exod. 9:29; 1 Kings 8:22; 2 Chron. 6:13). This practice was so common that it became a synonym for prayer in Psalm 141:2, "May my prayer be counted as incense before Thee; the lifting up of my hands as the evening offering." We infer that eyes were open during prayer from the statement that the publican would not "lift up his eyes to heaven" (Luke 18:13), and from the practice of Jesus Himself in looking up to heaven as He prayed (Mark 6:41; 7:34). The Bible does not speak of praying with eyes closed.[48]

For the converted Muslim, the most familiar prayer form is the "Dua"-style: hands raised to heaven, kneeling or sitting cross-legged and praying in his heart language. He will pray to Allah, the creator of heaven and hearth, in the name of Jesus the Messiah, a title for Jesus acknowledged by all Muslims.

➢ Worship style

It is crucial that God is worshiped. However, worship styles must find their cultural expressions.

Muslims are not permitted to accompany their worship with musical instruments. Verses from the Quran are often quoted rhythmically or with intonation.

These forms can be adapted: worship with rhythmical words, reading of psalms or hymns from the New Testament with the same intonation Islamic teachers use; worship through the proclamation of and the meditation on the 99 most beautiful names of God, reading of a creed or verses from the Word of God, especially the Psalms.

➢ Days and Times for Church Meetings

Although most Christians worldwide go to church on Sunday, there is no commandment in the Bible to do so. Of course we find biblical examples of believers that gathered on the first day of the week.

Though the New Testament urges believers not to abandon their gatherings, it does not specify a day or time for them.

> And let us consider how we may spur one another on towards love and good deeds. Let us not give up meeting together, as some are in the habit of doing, but let us encourage one another – and all the more as you see the Day approaching! (Hebrews 10:24-25)

Hesselgrave says:

> The writer to the Hebrews clearly stated that Christians should not neglect to assemble themselves together (Heb. 10:25). The primitive church followed the practice of meeting often. In fact, in the period after Pentecost, they met daily (Acts 2:46). It cannot be established, however, that there was one certain time when a congregation was required to meet. The Colossians were told not to allow anyone to judge them in regard to feast days or Sabbath days (Col. 2:16). The Romans were told that there was no agreement among Christians in regard to days (Rom. 14:5).[49]

For the Muslim prayer is only possible on Friday:

> O you who believe! When the call is proclaimed to prayer on Friday (the Day of Assembly), hasten earnestly to the Remembrance of Allah, and leave off activity (and traffic): That is best for you if ye but knew! (Sura 62:9)[50]

Therefore it is possible for the house church to gather for church on Friday. While Muslims attend the mosque, the converted Muslim also goes to pray – in the small house gathering just nearby.

As it is too risky for many Muslims to openly attend a Christian church, the possibility of nightly gatherings must be explored, too.

It must be emphasized again: It is not important *when* the church meets, but *that* the church meets. Meeting days and times should not be set by the church planter, but by the local believers.

- Meeting Place

Only a few Muslims could ever imagine entering a church. Converted Muslims should therefore meet in a contextual place, e.g. in a normal room of one of the house church members. Of course the word "church" in the biblical sense is defined by "the ones being called out" and not by "building." A church service should therefore be possible anywhere.

A Somali nomad once said "I am a Muslim, because all I need to pray is my mat, and I can pray anywhere. We see you Christians pray once a week, and this in a building. If you can strap your church building to the back of my camel, I will think that the Christian faith is relevant to us Somalis, too."

Contextual churches of the 11th hour have answers to such challenges, because they are highly flexible and adapt easily. To them a nomadic church that meets under trees, in hangers or tents poses no problem; an on-the-road Bible seminary for nomadic people by all means conceivable; elders without formal theological training administering the Lord's Supper possible; baptizing people through immersion in sand where there is no water absolutely justifiable.

They have learned to discern the substantial from the non-substantial. In substantial matters they adhere to the dogmatic. In non-substantial matters they are very flexible, always looking for contextual approaches.

2.8.6. Toward Insider Movements

Even the most contextualized churches may not lead to insider movements. Church planting often consists of the setting up of a new structure in a community, or alongside a community, and drawing people into it. Whether it is very Western or whether it incorporates forms familiar to the local people, even if the goal is to win whole families, these churches are essentially a new structure that displaces former forms of community fellowship, social welfare patterns, and authority structures. Insider movements are distinct from even rapidly spreading contextualized church planting movements in that in insider movements, the Gospel is spreading through *pre-existing* community networks.

2.9. Workers of the 11th hour are radically committed and highly flexible

The workers of the 11th hour resemble those of the 3rd hour in that, in New Testament times, flexibility was one of the most important requirements for a missionary.

Paul did seem to always have a strategy with clear cut goals, but those were frequently overthrown by the Holy Spirit (e.g. Acts 16: 6-15). Paul and his church planting team were highly flexible and always available for new assignments and changes of direction and strategy.

> He (Paul) did not start out with any definite design to establish his churches in this place or in that. He was led as God opened the door; but wherever he was led he always found a centre, and seizing upon that centre he made it a centre of Christian life.[51]

Mission was first and foremost living in the Kingdom of God with Jesus as its king. Jesus was Kyrios, the sole and sovereign Lord over their lives and thereby had the right to change their direction, to speak of new and surprising things and to lead them. Comfortable installation was a foreign word to them – in contrast, it was normal to be always on the road.

Jesus promised his disciples power to fulfil the Great Commission:

> But you will receive power when the Holy Spirit comes on you; and you will be my witnesses in Jerusalem, and in all Judea and Samaria, and to the ends of the earth (Acts 1:8).

The disciples would receive power to be witnesses. The Greek word here is "marturos," derived from "marturia" (witness). This word "undoubtedly means evangelistic confession and not just the testimony of blood. But it is the specific evangelistic confession that culminates in death."[52]

This word later became the English "martyr." So Jesus actually told his disciples: "You will receive the power of the Holy Spirit so that in your evangelistic witness you may live (a lifelong, sacrificial ministry) and die as martyrs (blood witness)."

And Jesus meant exactly what he said. Church history tells us that ten out of the twelve apostles were martyrs.[53]

The death of the first Apostles– The church historical tradition
❑ James was already beheaded by Herod in the year 44 ❑ Peter was crucified head down ❑ Andrew was crucified in Asia Minor in a X-shaped form ❑ Philip was murdered in Hierapolis ❑ Bartholomew was beaten to death in Armenia ❑ Thomas died as a martyr in India ❑ Matthew likewise in Ethiopia ❑ James was crucified in Egypt ❑ Thaddeus died as a martyr in Persia ❑ Simon was also crucified ❑ Paul that later joined the apostolic band, was imprisoned many times before being beheaded in Rome under Nero ❑ Only John died a natural death, but after a long imprisonment on Patmos

Table 6: The death of the first apostles according to church tradition

Paul tells us about his daily life in 2 Cor. 11:24-28:

> Five times I received from the Jews the forty lashes minus one. Three times I was beaten with rods, once I was stoned, three times I was shipwrecked, I spent a night and a day in the open sea, I have been constantly on the move. I have been in danger from rivers, in danger from bandits, in danger from my own countrymen, in danger from Gentiles; in danger in the city, in danger in the country, in danger at sea; and in danger from false brothers. I have laboured and toiled and have often gone without sleep; I have known hunger and thirst and have often gone without food; I have been cold and naked. Besides everything else, I face daily the pressure of my concern for all the churches.

And so it continued, decade after decade, century after century. Chapter 28 is not the end of Acts. It continues until this very day, until the Lamb is worshipped by all peoples. *But God has not changed his methods: His church is built through the suffering of his children.*

Modern societies try to avoid suffering at all cost. They find it deeply disturbing if a missionary is imprisoned or even killed.

But not so long ago things were different: the first missionaries that went to Africa took their own coffins with them, because they knew that 95% of them would not survive the first two years. During that time 19 out of 20 missionaries died within the first two years of ministry. If they did not end up in the pots of cannibals, they were victims of mosquitoes and died of malaria.

But still they went. Dozens. Hundreds. Thousands. Ready to lay down their lives for the Lamb.

Workers of the 11th hour view these New Testament experiences as normal, even as normative. For them, the willingness to suffer is daily bread, and many would consider it an honour to lay down their lives as martyrs.

Brother Yun presents his training manual for future Chinese missionaries:

> Each Back to Jerusalem missionary receives training in several main subjects. These include first: How to suffer and die for the Lord. We examine what the Bible says about suffering, and look at how the Lords people have laid down their lives for the advance of the gospel throughout history…[54]

In a more and more radical world, anything other than total, radical commitment would just not be enough to ultimately fulfil the Great Commission.

2.10. The workers of the 11th hour are the host of the final chapter

As mentioned above, throughout the centuries God has never been without witnesses. He always had a few individuals, at times even small groups, available to be his witnesses.

But to reach the masses of the 21st century, even a number of groups of workers are not enough. What is needed is a *host* of new workers. And this host can not be provided by the West, it requires the Global South.

While according to Johnstone[55] Europe has less than 20 million evangelical Christians, the rapidly growing church in China alone accounts for four times as many. The West African country of Nigeria has more evangelical Christians than all of Europe. The number of Brazilian evangelicals also exceeds 20 million.

To reach the billions of people of our generation, millions of workers are required. And this host of workers can be found nowhere else than in the Global South.

Without this host of workers, it will simply be impossible to fulfil the task.

The workers of the 11th hour will be sent individually, as worker have always been sent – but they will be so numerous that one cannot speak of sending individuals any more, but of *sending movements*.

These sending movements will face the two major challenges of the 21st century: to reach *all peoples,* and to penetrate the *mega-cities.*

2.10.1. All Unreached Peoples

Since the middle of the 20th century, the church has focussed more and more on the so called "hidden peoples." Although at the beginning of the 21st century there are no longer any *nations* without evangelical Christians, there are within the nations still many *people groups* without evangelical Christians.

According to Ralph Winter[56], there are 13,120 people groups world wide. Among them, in 1999 only 8,720 were reached; in other words: in two thousand years of mission history, the church of Christ managed to reach 8,720 different people groups with the gospel.

But there are still 4,400 people groups without an indigenous church. The largest bloc among them are the Muslim peoples (2,000 or

45.5%), followed by adherents of animist religions (1,400 people groups or 31.8%).

From a missiological and strategic perspective, it would be more useful to consider "cultural units" rather than "people groups", because within certain people groups cultural, linguistic and other differences of such magnitude are found that pioneering attempts with different strategies are required to reach the whole people group with indigenous church planting movements. If finer differences within specific people groups are taken into account, worldwide 24,000 different cultural units must be assumed, of which in 1999 still 10,000 were unreached.[57]

The workers of the 9th hour focussed first on coastal areas, then later on inland regions, and finally, in the second half of the 20th century, on unreached people groups, and they succeeded in planting churches among some of them. But the task remains for the host of the 11th hour to penetrate *all* peoples and *all* cultural units with church planting movements.

2.10.2. Mega-Cities

A massive unprecedented revolution of social structures has occurred within the last two centuries: the world population has migrated from rural areas into cities. "Two centuries ago the world was rural, with an urbanization of 4 % and only one mega-city in existence."[58] But this has changed quickly and radically:

> The twenty-first century will be an urban world, just as the previous 20 centuries of Christianity have been a rural world. The end of the second millennium is also the end of the rural majority with just over 50 % of the world's population urbanized....That trend will continue so that by 2100 the number of rural inhabitants may be only 10 % of the world's population.[59]

This trend is of such a magnitude that it equals a population movement: "The movement of more than a billion people to the cities over the last two decades is the largest population movement in history."[60]

The world wide church of Christ has not yet sufficiently responded to this radical shift. To date the church is still working within mostly rural structures and contexts.

Missionaries of the 9th hour were and still mostly are located in rural settings. They won rural areas, but lost urban centres. Dawson got it right when he said that we need:

> a new vision for Christian ministry. So far mission has always been associated with a romantic idyll, a picture of tribal peoples, palm trees and sunsets. We need to plant a new vision into the hearts of our young pioneering missionaries. Our new vision of missionary ministry must focus on the cities. If we want to win the nations for Christ, we need to conquer the cities.[61]

These urban centres are, next to the unreached people groups, the biggest missiological challenge for the church in the 21st century.

This goes along with Greenway:

> New people in the cities are open to new ideas, including ideas about God and religion. As a result, I have come to believe that God is behind the migration of masses of people to the cities. He is creating new opportunities for spreading the gospel among unreached people coming from remote towns and villages.... The migration to the cities is so large that it must have a divinely-ordained, redemptive purpose behind it.[62]

The host of the 11th hour has understood this new reality, because many of them were born and raised in mega-cities. Contrary to the workers of the 9th hour, they do not see these mega-cities as an evil threat, but as a God-given opportunity to spread the gospel.

At the beginning of the 21st century, there were 482 mega-cities (i.e. above one million people) and 20 super-cities (above 10 million people). The largest among them was Tokyo/Yokohama with 28 million people.[63]

The host of the 11th hour is a host of urban centres. To reach "the ends of the earth" may mean for many of them to move into one of the countless slums or quarters of a mega-city.

Working within traditional structures, workers of the 9th hour have planted *some churches* in mega-cities. But it remains for the host of the 11th hour to literally *flood* all mega-cities with house church movements.

ENDNOTES

1 Patrick Johnstone and Jason Mandryk, *Operation World*, p. 21.

2 Jonathan J. Bonks, *Mission and Money*, p. 60.

3 Johnstone and Mandryk, op. cit, pp. 485 & 489.

4 Ruth E. Siemens, "Tentmakers Needed for World Evangelization," in *Perspectives on the World Christian Movement*, ed. Ralph D. Winter and Steven C. Hawthorne, p. 736.

5 Alfred Kuen, ed., *Nouveau Dictionnaire Biblique*, p. 1021.

6 Siemens, op. cit., p. 738

7 Siemens, ibid., p. 739.

8 Siemens in *Perspectives on the World Christian Movement*, p. 739.

9 William D. Taylor, "Examining the Iceberg called Attrition," in *Too Valuable to Lose*, ed. William D. Taylor, p. 13.

10 Robert J. Clinton, *The Making of a Leader*, p. 77.

11 Ibid., p. 83.

12 Kenneth Williams, " A Model for Mutual Care in Missions," in *Missionary Care*, ed. Kelly O'Donnell, p. 58.

13 David J. Hesselgrave, "Culture-Sensitive Counseling and the Christian Mission," in *Helping Missionaries Grow*, ed. Kelly O'Donnell, p. 533.

14 Duane Elmer, *Cross-Cultural Conflict*, pp. 63-134.

15 Daryl Platt, "A Call to Partnership in the Missionary Selection Process," in *Too Valuable to Lose*, op. cit., p. 203.

16 chemed.chem.purdue.edu/genchem/glossary/c.html

17 Adapted from Frontiers-GI-brochure, 2004.

18 Peter Batchelor, *People in Rural Development*, p. 42-43.

19 Roland Bunch, *Two Ears of Corn*, p. 36.

[20] George Verwer, *Out of the Comfort Zone*, p. 99.

[21] Sherwood Lingenfelter, *Transforming Culture*, p. 15.

[22] Sherwood G. Lingenfelter and Marvin K. Mayers, *Ministering Cross-Culturally*, p. 21.

[23] Ibid. pp. 33-102.

[24] Lothar Käser, *Fremde Kulturen*, p. 242.

[25] Sobhi Malek, *Islam: Challenge and Mandate*, ch. 13.

[26] Rick Love, *Muslims, Magic and the Kingdom of God*, p. 120.

[27] Rick Warren, *Kirche mit Vision (The Purpose-Driven Church)*, p. 208.

[28] David J. Hesselgrave, *Communicating Christ Cross-Culturally*, p. 536.

[29] Greg Livingstone, *Planting Churches in Muslim Cities*, pp. 142-145.

[30] David Garrison, *Church Planting Movements*, p. 7.

[31] Livingstone, op. cit., p. 162.

[32] Garrison, op. cit., pp. 33-36.

[33] Melvin L. Hodges, *A Guide to Church Planting*, p. 108.

[34] Kenneth S. Latourette, *Missions Tomorrow*, p. 159.

[35] Geoffrey W. Bromiley, *Theological Dictionary of the New Testament*, p. 674.

[36] Ralph W. Neighbour, *Where Do We Go From Here?* pp. 117-118.

[37] Dick Scoggins, *Planting House Churches in Networks*, p. 47.

[38] John D. Robb, *Focus! The Power of People Group Thinking*, p. 25.

[39] Donald A. McGavran, *Understanding Church Growth*, pp. 297-298.

[40] Love, op. cit., p. 112.

[41] John Wimber, *Allez.... Guérissez*, p. 172.

[42] Henrietta C. Mears, *Panorama du Nouveau Testament*, p. 226.

[43] C. Peter Wagner, *Acts of the Holy Spirit*, p. 240.

[44] Wolfgang Simson, *Häuser, die die Welt verändern*, p. 108.

[45] Groupes Bibliques Universitaires, *Les Communautés de Maison*, p. 15.

[46] Garrison, op. cit., p. 35.

[47] Simson, Häuser, op. cit., p. 109.

[48] Phil Parshall, *New Paths in Muslim Evangelism*, ch. 9.

[49] David J. Hesselgrave, *Planting Churches Cross-Culturally*, p. 293.

[50] La Présidence Générale des Directions des Recherches Scientifiques Islamiques, *Le Saint Coran*, p. 554.

[51] Roland Allen, *Missionary Methods: St. Paul's or Ours?* p. 17.

[52] Bromiley, op. cit., pp. 568-569.

[53] Charles Thompson, *La Bible Thompson*, p. 1709.

[54] Brother Yun and Paul Hattaway, *The Heavenly Man*, p. 290.

[55] Johnstone and Mandryk, op. cit., p. 52.

[56] Ralph D. Winter and Bruce A. Koch, " Finishing the Task," in *Perspectives on the World Christian Movement*, ed. Ralph D. Winter and Steven C. Hawthorne, p. 521.

[57] Ibid.

[58] Patrick Johnstone, *The Church is Bigger Than You Think*, p. 241.

[59] Ibid., pp. 241-242.

[60] Roger S. Greenway, "The Challenge of the Cities," in *Perspectives on the World Christian Movement*ed. Ralph D. Winter and Steven C. Hawthorne, p. 553.

[61] John Dawson, *Conquérir nos villes pour Dieu*, p. 21.

[62] Greenway in op. cit., pp. 554-555 and 557.

[63] Johnstone and Mandryk, op. cit., p. 1.

CHAPTER 3

THE ELEVEN PARTNERSHIP MODELS

Flexibility is the precept of the present time in an ever changing world. Whereas there were only a few different models of missionary work in the early phases of modern mission, the workers of the eleventh hour are characterized by a multitude of very different models, methods and strategies.

However, the goal remains the same: to mobilize masses of new workers through indigenous sending structures that lead to evangelism and planting of churches that plant churches themselves (the so-called Church Planting Movement).

In this chapter, we will present some of the patterns of the eleventh hour that are already applied in different parts of the world. In doing so, we don't claim to be exhaustive. On the contrary, we are convinced that while growing and maturing, the host of the eleventh hour will develop ever more new and effective models.

Partnership is the key word for missions in the 21st century.

> More so than ever before mission is a global, cooperative movement. We have to be prepared for new partnerships, new insights, and new approaches by non-Western mission structures. At the same time we need to recognize that the western missionary story is a reservoir of mission experience that can serve the emerging missions.[1]

Global partnership means the involvement of the whole, worldwide body of Christ for the sake of reaching the whole world. A valid partnership is characterized by both parties being involved according to their gifting and strength. They work complementarily, respecting each other and focusing on achieving synergy.

All of the eleven models presented in this chapter are therefore partnership models between two equal partners: the church of the Global North and the church of the Global South. In doing so the church of the Global North accepts that the emerging movements of the Global South must develop *their* own structures, implement *their* own strategies, follow *their* own leaders and bear *their* own name. The Northern churches must accept that they are no longer parents of underage children, but partners with mature, adult counterparts.

We will present each model using a case study and will examine each in three specific areas: background, strategy and financial support. For security reasons there will be no mention of names and locations.

3.1. The "Partnering in Tentmaking" Model

3.1.1. Background

This partnership model is applied in two neighboring West African countries. The southern country has a rapidly growing evangelical church, whereas the population of the neighboring country is almost a 100% Islamic. A church in this country has been planted, but is very small and almost invisible.

These countries have a lot in common despite numerous differences: they share the same language and use only different dialects. There are almost no cultural differences. Strong evangelical churches of the southern country are in some cases separated only by a few dozen miles from completely un-churched areas of the northern country. And even though different people groups live along the borders, they still share the same trade language.

The small church in the northern country is fighting for its survival and can hardly imagine reaching out to the unreached people groups in its own country. However, during the last years the big and growing church in the country to the South went through a tough time of hardship and persecution. Hundreds of believers died as martyrs. This suffering prepared the church to proclaim the gospel boldly and fearlessly.

3.1.2 Strategy

In 2001 a partnership was formed between a western mission organization and one of the strongest evangelical mission movements of the southern country. All the principles outlined in chapter 2 were followed and dependency was avoided.

The evangelical church of the southern country was involved in selecting and training the missionaries. Only missionaries who had already been working fruitfully in their home country were selected. All of them were married and had children.

The African sending movement committed itself to support these workers through a monthly allowance that should cover about 50% of their living expenses. This is roughly the equivalent to the support they give to their other missionaries that do church planting in their home country. However, a missionary working in another country needs around twice as much as one working in the home country.

The mission organization from the West contributed in the following areas:

- Provided suitable housing for the missionary family and a potential initial meeting place for the believers (normally in the missionary's yard).
- Financed the tentmaker activity, usually a farming project (cows, ploughs) or a micro-enterprise.
- Coached and mentored the missionaries through competent and experienced local leaders.

Whereas the African partner contributed to this endeavour on a monthly basis, the Western partner sponsored through one-time contributions.

3.1.3. Financial Support

The missionary's support came from two sources:

- A monthly allowance from the African sending movement
- Earnings from his tentmaker activity

After the initial set up of the missionary's ministry, there was no more western money involved.

3.2. THE DISTRICT MODEL

3.2.1. Background

In this country in Central Africa, the missionaries and the people group they are working with do not share a common language, but are geographically proximate: they all live in the same district of the same country.

In this district, there are around 20 different people groups totalling about 500,000 people.

A couple of decades ago, churches were planted among two of these people groups. Yet, in 2004, there were still 13 people groups with more than 1,000 members unreached.

Although the people groups with existing churches and the ones without do not speak the same tribal language, they are certainly proximate: they are culturally related, have a similar lifestyle (clothing, etc.), live off the same activities (farming), and speak the same trade language (Arabic)

3.2.2. Strategy

Despite their small membership, the little denomination of this district committed itself to select and send over the next eight years the 13 missionaries that would be necessary to start a church planting ministry among each unreached people group in their region.

As they live within the same district, they were able to identify the priority groups that needed to be reached most urgently. The church appointed a missions leader who visits and coaches the missionaries.

The Western partner complements the church in this district through missiological training at the local Bible school and by teaching at conferences for mission candidates and already on-site missionaries.

Additionally, the Western partner funds the expenses for the initial tentmaker activity through a one-time contribution and a small monthly allowance comprising 40% of the living expenses during the first six months, 33% during the next six months, and 25% in the second year. The monthly allowances end after four years.

3.2.3. Financial Support

Support is provided in two stages:

- In the first four years: partial support comes from the western partner in addition to the earnings from the tentmaker activity.
- After four years: support is provides exclusively by the missionary's tentmaker activity.

As the missionary continues to live in his district, there is no reason to support him financially long term. His normal method of earning a living before the move should also provide for him in his new location after a reasonable period of adjustment.

3.3. The Government Model

3.3.1. Background

A country in Central Africa is characterized by a discrepancy between the South and the North. In the South, the soil is fruitful and the population is Christian, poor, and educated. In the North, vegetation is scarce and the people are Muslim, wealthier, but less educated. In this country, the government is secular.

There are government schools and hospitals all over the northern part of the country where totally unreached people groups live.

However, as the people groups of the South are more educated than their northern country men, they make up most of the government officials. About one million of these people are Christian, and many of them are employed by the government.

However, most of the government officials view a transfer to the North as a punishment or exile, as this part of the country is rougher and hotter and they would be hundreds of miles away from their extended family.

3.3.2. Strategy

One denomination in this country has started to increase missions awareness in their churches. They are specifically recruiting their members who are government officials.

The western partner helps in training these candidates at special events and conferences.

After receiving this training, these church members ask the government for a transfer to the North. As there are hardly any employees volunteering for such an assignment, it is almost certain that the request is granted. And so a teacher or doctor can work and minister in the North funded and protected by the government.

3.3.3. Financial Support

The worker is a 100% funded by the government. No local sending church or western partner contributes to his living expenses.

3.4. THE TRUST MODEL

3.4.1. Background

This Trust Model is practiced in an Asian country. Its population is 80% Muslim with over 200 unreached people groups. Yet, in the same country live also millions of evangelical Christians who belong to many different denominations.

3.4.2. Strategy

A local denomination and a western partner founded a trust to finance the ministry of local tentmakers.

The western partner acted as an adviser in the foundation of the trust. He also models missiological principles such as contextualization and trains future missionaries that will be commissioned by the trust.

The leadership of the local partner is responsible for the funding of the trust. The fundraising is done within and outside the country.

3.4.3. Financial Support

The trust supports the missionaries by funding the initial set-up of their tentmaker activity and through small monthly allowances. The trust itself receives money from local and foreign partners that use this structure to finance the missionaries indirectly.

3.5. The Three Part model

3.5.1. Background

The area around the big lake is very fruitful. It is for this reason and the resulting prosperity that many different people groups have moved here. Although the indigenous population is 100% Muslim consisting of various language and ethnic groups, many of the migrated people are evangelical or nominal Christians.

As a result some informal cell groups of migrated Christians have began to meet for prayer and Bible study – without any missionary residing there.

3.5.2. Strategy

Missionaries that have so far worked in another part of the country earning their living through farming are selected by an indigenous denomination. In the beginning, the western partner supports 25% of their living expenses.

3.5.3. Financial Support

The support consists of three parts:

- The local cell group of evangelical Christians (25%)
- The western partner (25%, gradually reduced over four years to 0%)
- Earnings of the missionary through his job as a tentmaker

In a slightly modified version, it is the indigenous church in another part of the country that plays the role of the local partner instead of the cell group at the location. This could be a comparatively rich church, in the capital for example, where many of the members are government officials or otherwise people with good income. They would be able to support the missionary with 25% of his expenses. As this is local money, there is no objection for the support to be continued over a long period of time, especially if the missionary's tentmaker activity doesn't develop as well as he had hoped for.

3.6. THE STOCKBREEDING MODEL

3.6.1. Background

To illustrate this model we will look at two different case studies.

Most of the members of one specific unreached people group in West Africa make their living as stock breeders raising small livestock like goats, sheep, and chicken.

The other example comes from East Africa where an unreached people group mainly lives by farming. This is, however, limited to the rainy season and done without the use of modern technology.

3.6.2. Strategy

In West Africa: At his commissioning service the missionary receives small livestock (e.g., a pair of goats) from his home church as a gift, as well as the money he needs for the journey to his future ministry location.

In East Africa: At his commissioning service the missionary receives two cows and a plow.

3.6.3. Financial Support

The support of the missionary consists of the small livestock given to him at the beginning of his ministry. The home church assumes that they will multiply and provide enough income to cover all the expenses. No Western money is involved.

In East Africa: The tentmaker lives off of his cows in several ways:

- During the rainy season his cows help him to farm a larger field, as his plow enables him to work more effectively and much faster.
- He also plows the fields of other villagers during this season who hire him for the day.
- During the dry season he uses his cows and a small carriage to transport goods for the villagers from the market.
- As the cows grow bigger, he will sell them off after 1-2 years and buy other, younger cows with part of the money he gained.

The entire support consists of the initial tentmaker set-up. No western money is involved. A variation of the model would be a partnership with a Western sponsor who provides part of the needed initial equipment.

3.7. The Multiple Church Model

3.7.1. Background

This is the situation in one of the poorest countries in Africa. Through the labour of workers of the 9th hour, a lot of churches have been planted in various districts of the country. However, there are regions in other parts that are Muslim and totally unreached by the message of the gospel.

3.7.2. Strategy

All churches in a district with a strong evangelical presence adopt an unreached people group in a neighboring district. This proximate district assumes the responsibility for the new worker.

3.7.3. Financial Support

There is no western money involved in this model. Depending on the situation, several possibilities are possible:

- "Tithe of tithes": A monthly financial gift consists of the tithes of all the offerings of the churches in the Christian district. However, this strategy almost never works in poor rural areas.
- A one-time investment into the tentmaker activity: the whole district calls for a one-time offering that funds the necessary equipment for the new missionary.
- An offering collected at harvest time: in rural areas harvest time is the best season for offerings. The churches in the district can share a part of their harvest with the missionary.
- The missionary's field: each church in the district labors on one specific field as a community. Any profits of that field are then given to the missionary.

3.8. THE MORAVIAN MODEL

3.8.1. Background

The background for this model is not contemporary, but rather historical: the missionary movement of the Moravians. It was established by the Count of Zinzendorf and was probably the biggest protestant missions movement in the 18th century.

3.8.2. Strategy

The Moravian model is very similar to the one Paul used in Corinth. A team is made up of several tentmakers, each one working according to his or her ability or training.

> All of them were craftsmen, one a carpenter, another a potter. They had received good training in the schools in Herrnhut and were gifted preachers. They started out on foot taking with them no more baggage than they could carry on their backs.... Their devotion to Christ compelled them to head especially for areas where the work would be the hardest and most dangerous.[2]

Tucker writes the following regarding the Moravian missions movement:

> All of these missionaries were lay men, not trained as theologians, but as evangelists. As lay people and used to provide for them they were expected to work in manual labour alongside the people they wanted to minister to. They were witnesses to their faith through sharing the word and living it out, always eager to identify themselves with the people rather than to see themselves as superior to them.[3]

Their dedication and willingness to suffer were an example:

> Many of their members were craftsmen or had acquired other skills or were merchants. This gave them the opportunity to work in other parts of the world. Often they would set off in groups of two or three after having discerned the mind of the Lord and received assurance to which place He would want to lead them. There they settled, learned the language, the specific customs and way of life. They opened a activity and whatever they did shared their faith and gathered in fellowships the ones that had come to believe. Often they would share the same faith with those they had come to minister to. They suffered persecution, were willingly sold into slavery to be able to bring the gospel to other slaves, were slaughtered together with the American Indian among which they lived in North America. All this is part of the heritage of the Moravian brotherhood. Many of them died as martyrs.[4]

Yet, whenever the missions movement of the Moravians is mentioned, one must also point out the important ministry of prayer and intercession that was without any doubt a central part of Zinzendorf's strategy.

Another quote by Tucker:

> There was a mighty sense of unity and absolute dependence on God. A prayer movement was launched that led people to pray 24

hours a day, seven days in the week for more than one hundred years without ceasing.[5]

3.8.3. Financial Support

These teams of tentmakers received no external support, except in some cases the necessary resources to set up the tentmaker activity. Usually tentmakers set off carrying with them the equipment they had already used before to establish themselves at a new place while proclaiming their message.

3.9. THE NEIGHBORHOOD MODEL

3.9.1. Background

This is a typical situation in a capital of the Global South. The population is about one million people. Here, like in many other capitals, Christians and Muslims live in the same quarters and have a normal relationship as neighbors do. Churches and mosques are often not more than 150 yards apart. The relations between members of the different religions are polite, but not warm; not hostile, but also not friendly.

3.9.2. Strategy

Through various courses at Bible schools and church events, Christians are trained to make friends with their Muslim neighbors and share the Good News with them. They are taught how to live as good neighbors, living a lifestyle of sacrificial service: doing good to their neighbors, praying with them in the name of Jesus when they are in need and sick, being hospitable, etc.

In particular, the Christians are taught to live contextually in all areas of their lives, thus avoiding all unnecessary barriers to their Muslim neighbors. They are taught not to invite Muslim seekers to their church services, but rather into their own homes, making them the center of the activity. In this way meetings start and "church" is happening without anyone noticing it.

3.9.3. Financial Support

No support is necessary – ordinary church members are already working as tentmakers but add the role of missionaries. They continue working in their jobs, but at the same time consider themselves evangelists to their Muslim neighbors, intentionally spending time with them, being hospitable, serving them practically and proclaiming the gospel through their daily lives in word and deed.

3.10. The Globalization Model

3.10.1. Background

The present day trend of globalization opens up new and more effective possibilities for the body of Christ to plant churches in countries that have so far been closed to the gospel and have not granted missionary visas.

The Arab Peninsula is a good example for this model. It is absolutely impossible to reside and work officially as a missionary in one of these countries, let alone do church planting. To work as a tentmaker is the only possible strategy.

The United Arab Emirates serve as a useful example:

> Dubai is an important commercial, information technology and industrial center. The UAE's great economic dilemma is its complete dependence on cheap foreign labour.[6]

There is no way for Dubai to survive economically without foreign workers.

Siemens states the following:

> For almost 20 years, our Global Opportunities staff laboriously researched overseas jobs, turning up about 3000 a month. But today 60,000 or 70,000 jobs can be accessed on the Internet a day! Thousands of employers (about 40 kinds) hire people in every career field for positions in cities everywhere, as well as some rural and tribal locations.[7]

There are currently more Christians of different backgrounds on the Arab Peninsula than ever before. Bahrain's population, for example, is 10.4% Christian, growing at an annual rate of 3.4%. Among these are 19,000 evangelical Christians representing 3.1% of Bahrain's total population.[8] This is even more amazing considering that Europe by comparison has a meager 2.4% of evangelicals!

In Saudi-Arabia, the undisputed center of Islam, there are about one million at least nominal Christians. Estimates suggest that around 188,000 or 0.9% of the total population are evangelicals. Most of them are Philippines, Indians, and Nigerians.[9] If only one in a hundred considered himself as a missionary, there would be almost 2,000 in Saudi-Arabia!

These facts are unique in the history of missions and should not be overlooked any longer by the body of Christ! The Lord himself has sent his host of harvesters right into the midst of the strongholds of Islam – because now is the harvest time!

3.10.2. Strategy

Churches from the Global South are looking for job offers in the Middle East and specifically on the Arabian Peninsula on the Internet or by other means.

The tentmakers are then selected according to their training, professional expertise or natural gifting. They can be highly qualified (e.g. medical doctors, engineers, professors, IT experts) or unqualified (e.g. sweepers, domestic servants, bricklayers).

The kind of secular job that gets him or her the entry visa is not crucial. But it is crucial that they are conscious of their missionary calling and go with the determination to plant churches.

Western partners may help in training and coaching. As they have been practicing this model already since several years, they can offer valuable experience and insight to others.

However, it is crucial to stress the importance of training for the evangelical Christians from the Global South already now living in the Middle East. Many of those came to these countries primarily not for missionary, but economical reasons. Yet, with God nothing happens by chance. Through careful and anointed training, many of these Christians will realize their real calling and start an intentional church planting ministry.

Evangelical Christians may secretly organize an underground conference or trainings event and invite an experienced tentmaker to teach them in church planting.

3.10.3. Financial Support

No support by the sending church or a western partner is needed. However, there might be the need to cover the initial travel expenses in some cases.

The worker is 100% funded by the employer in his host country.

3.11. The Traditional Model

3.11.1. Background

In recent years, some urban areas in the Global South have experienced an enormous economical growth and their living standard can compare with the one in the West.

Though this model is presented at the end of our list, we believe that it is still valuable for the future, especially if the wealthier urban churches increasingly catch the vision for the yet unreached people groups that are proximate to them.

3.11.2. Strategy

This is the strategy usually applied in the West: A *local* church, group or denomination commissions a missionary and takes full financial and other responsibility for him.

3.11.3. Financial Support

The home church provides all of the financial support, but even in this model a combination of church support and income through a tentmaking activity is preferable.

3.12. Is the Jesus Model a model of the 11th hour?

The Jesus–Model differs from all other models. It is simpler. It is more God-centered. It needs less structure and fewer organizations. It is highly effective. But it requires an enormous amount of faith and boldness.

It is presented to us in the Gospel of Luke:

> After this the Lord appointed seventy-two others and sent them two by two ahead of him to every town and place where he was about to go. 'Go! I am sending you out like lambs among wolves. Do not take a purse or bag or sandals; and do not greet anyone on the road. When you enter a house, first say, 'Peace to this house.' If a man of peace is there, your peace will rest on him; if not, it will return to you. Stay in that house, eating and drinking whatever they give you, for the worker deserves his wages. Do not move around from house to house. When you enter a town and are welcomed, eat what is set before you. Heal the sick who are there and tell them, 'The Kingdom of God is near you' (Luke 10:1, 3-9).

They will be among the host of the 11th hour, those followers of Jesus who will go in groups of two or three and led by the Holy Spirit to those towns and villages where the Lord is about to go. They will set out without financial support, without any supporting technology, without sophisticated means of transport, bringing with them only the things they can carry. Led by the Holy Spirit, they will identify the men of peace and women of honour that will extend hospitality to them. They will be the real insiders who will reach the society with the message of the gospel from inside out.

Once these men of peace have repented and follow Jesus, they, as the heads of households and cultural insiders, will share the gospel in a contextual way with their women and children. Whole families will come to Christ and a house church will be formed. This house church will then apply the same model to plant other house churches in other parts of the town, or in other villages of the area. This will eventually lead to a house church movement that will penetrate the whole mega city or people group with the Gospel.

These disciples will bring with them the divine Shalom manifesting itself through the coming of God's kingdom when they teach with authority followed by healings and acts of deliverance.

We find this same model in the book of Acts in chapter eight where we read about unplanned, but very effective multiplication and exponential church growth:

> On that day a great persecution broke out against the church at Jerusalem, and all the apostles were scattered throughout Judea and Samaria. Those who had been scattered preached the word wherever they went (Acts 8:1-4).
> Now those who had been scattered by the persecution in connection with Stephen travelled as far as Phoenicia, Cyprus and Antioch, telling the message only to Jews (Acts 11:19).

This multiplication happened through ordinary members of the church. Driven out due to persecution, having lost their possessions, they literally flooded large areas, preaching the gospel and planting new churches. They even reached influential centers like Antioch!

Conclusions

The following table summarizes the eleven partnership models of the 11th hour.

Christians from the West tend to underestimate the potential of the churches in the Global South or fail to take them seriously.

From a theological perspective, poverty does not release a people from contributing towards the fulfilment of the Great Commission. In missions history, especially in the case of the workers of the 3rd hour who have taken the gospel to many unreached areas,

Model	Background	Strategy	Financial Support
"Partnering in Tentmaker" Model	Two neighboring countries; cultural, economical and language proximity. Strong churches in one country, unreached areas in the other	Tentmakers are chosen and sent out by strong churches in the one country. Western partner sponsors housing, equipment for tentmaker job and coaching	Monthly support through sending African church Income from tentmaker job.
District Model	Geographical and cultural proximity, no language similarities; within the same country	Western partner trains tentmakers in one-off events; sponsors the equipment of the tentmaker; missionaries selected, sent and coached by local partner	During the first years partially supported by the Western partner; income from tentmaker job.
Government Model	Christian South, Islamic North; many government officials are evangelical Christians	Evangelical government officials are transferred to the North by the government	100 % by the government
Trust Model	Within the same country; millions of evangelicals – many unreached Muslim people groups	Western partner helps to found the trust and in training	Supporters inside and outside the country donate money to the trust that funds tentmaker equipment and a minimal regular support.
The Three-Part Model	Believers and unreached people live side by side; non-indigenous cell groups on site	A tentmaker is sent out	Existing cell groups; income from tentmaker job; western partner sponsors max. 25%, reduced to 0% over 4 years
The Stockbreeding Model	Unreached people group make their living from farming or raising cattle	Tentmaker receives a couple of goats or cows	Goats multiply; cows are used to plough the fields, as means of transports, are being hired out
Multiple Church Model	Within the same country; districts with numerous churches next to districts without any church	A whole district adopts an unreached people group in a neighboring district that has no churches	All churches of one district support the tentmaker jointly; district collects offerings, financial and/or material goods
Moravian Model	Worldwide missions movement of the Moravians in the 18th century	Craftsmen working in teams take their equipment to unreached areas, they work in their profession and evangelize at the same time	Through their tentmaker activity
Neighbour-hood Model	Mega-City; Christians and Muslims live side-by-side in the same part of town as neighbors	One-time training events and conferences; Christians realize their calling to reach their M. neighbors through contextual living	No support; Christians living out visibly the gospel message of love towards their neighbors
Globalisation Model	In the time of globalization and high mobility anyone can find a job anywhere	Evangelical Christians look for jobs in restricted access areas through the Internet	Provided a 100 % through the employer in the host country
Traditional Model	Well developed urban areas	Local church or denomination commissions their missionaries	Provided a 100 % through the local sending church or denomination
Jesus-Model?	everywhere	Ordinary lay people go two-by-two into unreached areas trusting solely on God	No support; trusting in God's provision; hospitality provided by men of peace

Table 7: The eleven partnership models of the 11th hour

missionaries have often been poor people. From a missiological perspective, it is much more effective if the missionary shares the living standard of the people he is trying to reach, even more so if his tentmaker activity is identical with the main source of income of the people to be reached.

The main goal of this chapter was to prove that there are indeed possibilities of working together in partnership to release the potential of the Global South. In some cases an initial support from the outside might be necessary to get started – but even so, it can be handled in a way that long-term dependency is avoided and multiplication remains possible.

The western church must never forget that the time of paternalism is over. We are dealing with equal partners who themselves bear responsibility before God to be good stewards of their resources and opportunities.

If we don't allow the church of the Global South to participate financially in the great mission enterprise of God, we will rob them of the great blessings of God. God's truth that "it is more blessed to give than to receive" (Acts 20:35) applies to them as well. And for them also it is possible to put God to the test whether he will bless them when they bring into his house the tithe in its fullness (Mal. 3:10). Jesus' words are true for them that it will be measured to them according the measure they use (Luke 6:38b).

In the final analysis, paternalism is sin – a social sin towards our precious brothers and sisters that are now mature and who *in their own right and sacred duty* must invest all of their spiritual, human, *financial and material resources* to participate in the completion of the great cause. And that, indeed, is what they desire as this quote of an African leader proves:

> God's church in Africa is of age to support missions. We have received so much in the past. It is time for us to evangelise whatever is left in our continent.[10]

Endnotes

[1] Ralph D. Winter and Bruce A. Koch, "Finishing the Task," in *Perspectives on the World Christian Movement,* ed. Ralph D. Winter and Steven C. Hawthorne, p. 523.

[2] E. H. Broadbent, *Gemeinde Jesu in Knechtsgestalt (The Pilgrim Chruch),* p. 268.

[3] Ruth A. Tucker, *Aux extrémités de la terre*, p. 81.

[4] Dick Scoggins, *Planting House Churches in Networks,* pp. 10-11.

[5] Tucker, op. cit., p. 80.

[6] Patrick Johnstone and Jason Mandryk, *Operation World,* p. 647.

[7] Ruth E. Siemens, "Tentmakers Needed for World Evangelization," in *Perspectives on the World Christian Movement*, ed. Ralph D. Winter and Steven C. Hawthorne, p. 736.

[8] Johnstone and Mandryk, op. cit., pp. 92-93.

[9] Ibid, p. 556.

[10] Obed Uzodinma, *Mobilising Churches in Africa for Missions,* p. 69.

Chapter 4

Three Visions of the Final Chapter

Over and over again, the Lord of the harvest has given visions to his workers. Often they would wrestle in secret with God who wanted to entrust them with a commission. They felt weak and unable to take up the great calling. Yet, God rejoices when he can glorify himself in his children that in their helplessness trust him completely.

Hudson Taylor was one of them. As an old man having ministered for 51 fruitful years in China, he repeated over and over again this important sentence: "It is possible to trust the Lord too little, but it is never possible to trust him too much!"[1]

For the last chapter of world mission the Lord has given visions to his people as well:

4.1. Vision 5:9

Vision 5:9 takes its name from the great vision of the end of times recorded in Rev. 5:9:

> And they sang a new song: 'You are worthy to take the scroll and to open its seals, because you were slain, and with your blood you purchased men for God from every tribe and language and people and nation.'

Vision 5:9 is therefore a call to all mission organizations and churches to work tirelessly and invest all necessary means towards the realization of this end time vision – when people from *all* ethnic groups will gather before the throne of the Lamb.

Vision 5:9 is a movement of partnerships between some of the largest evangelical missions working among Muslim peoples. The aim of this interdenominational and worldwide partnership is to create momentum through coordinated efforts that will send workers into all unreached people groups in the world. No matter whether they are sent from the Global North or the Global South.

4.2. VISION 2025

Vision 2025 derives its name from the year 2025.

Influential leaders of some larger evangelical mission organizations have the impression that the fulfilment of the Great Commission can be achieved within our generation.

> We are in the final era of missions. For the first time in history it is possible to see the end of the tunnel when there will be a church movement within the language and social structure of every people group on earth, powerful face to face evangelism taking over in all peoples. God is moving throughout His global body to fulfil His promise to the nations in ways that we could not possibly have imagined 20 years ago.[2]

The task that is yet unfinished has become tangible. Worldwide missiological research has shown how many ethnic groups still need to be reached and where they live.

> For the first time in history we have a reasonably complete listing of the world's peoples and the extent to which they have been evangelized.[3]

Through international partnerships within the body of Christ, there are now ministries established or soon to be started in almost all people groups with a population of more than 10,000. For this reason Johnstone concludes optimistically:

> The implications of this are immense and exciting. It means that we are also running out of peoples where there is no pioneer work already in progress or in planning. To have reached this point is a very special moment in the history of missions![4]

However, this excludes around a 1,000 people groups that consist of less than 10,000 people, but are nevertheless strategic for pioneer missions.

> Now, in the 1990's, the completion of the greatest project in history is within sight. It's determined that the Church has the necessary information, the necessary resources, and the necessary manpower to send church-planting teams to every remaining unreached people group on earth.... Blasting through the remaining tasks involved in this cosmic enterprise will not be easy; there will be blood, sweat, tears, and body counts. But, in the 1890's words of the evangelist D.L. Moody, "It can be done. It must be done!"[5]

It is therefore the goal of strategic partnerships to launch church planting efforts and Bible translating teams among all unreached people groups within the next few years.

Vision 2025 is basically Vision 5:9 spelled out in a time frame: there should be no more unreached people group by the year 2025.

4.3. Vision 9-11

Since 2001 and the horrendous terror attacks in the US, the abbreviation 9-11 means terror and war.

However, there is still another Vision 9-11 than the one of terror. It is the vision of Jesus who talks about it in this parable:

> When evening came, the owner of the vineyard said to his foreman, 'Call the workers and pay them their wages, beginning with the last ones hired and going on to the first.' The workers who were hired about the eleventh hour came and each received a denarius. So when those came who were hired first, they expected to receive more. But each one of them also received a denarius (Mt. 20:8-10).

The workers of the 9th hour and those of the 11th hour will each receive their due wages. They will join in with the workers of the early morning and the ones of the 3rd and 6th hour.

Vision 9-11 takes its name from the due wages that all the workers will receive. There won't be one receiving more or one receiving less. All of them have worked diligently and with much commitment

– some of them for a shorter, some for a longer period of time; some have suffered more, some less; some have seen much fruit, some little; some had more resources at their disposal, some less.

At this day, however, this will all fall into oblivion. One thing only will be important, no matter in what missiological era one ministered, what skin color he or she had or how many churches he or she had planted. Only one thing will count: the Lord of the harvest telling his worker:

> You have been faithful with a few things; I will put you in charge of many things. *Come and share your master's happiness* (Mt. 25:23b, italics added).

This is our vision for the end of times:

- All unreached people groups are reached by church planting teams.
- All people groups gathered before the throne to worship the Lamb together.
- All workers rewarded with eternal happiness by the Lord of the harvest.

That is what we are working towards; with all our efforts, with highest commitment and willingness to sacrifice whatever necessary, in partnership with the worldwide body of Christ, to the glory of the Lamb and ultimately that the Lord the Almighty might be worshipped by all peoples!

ENDNOTES

1 John W. Cowart, *People Whose Faith Got Them into Trouble,* p. 120.

2 Ralph D. Winter and Bruce A. Koch, "Finishing the Task," in *Perspectives on the World Christian Movement,* ed. Ralph D. Winter and Steven C. Hawthorne, p. 523.

3 Patrick Johnstone, *The Church is Bigger Than You Think,* p. 229.

4 Ibid, p. 229.

5 Bill and Amy Stearns, *Catch the Vision 2000,* p. 140.

Bibliography

Allen, Roland. *Missionary Methods: St. Paul's or Ours?* Grand Rapids: Eerdmans, 1962.

Batchelor, Peter. *People in Rural Development*. Exeter: Paternoster, 1981.

Bonks, Jonathan J. *Missions and Money: Affluence as a Western Missionary Problem*. Maryknoll: Orbis, 2003.

Broadbent, E. H. *Cremeinde Jesu in Knechtsgestalt (The Pilgrim Church)*. Dillenburg: Christliche Verlagsgesell Schaft, 1987.

Bromiley, Geoffrey W. *Theological Dictionary of the New Testament*. Grand Rapids: Eerdmans, 1990.

Bunch, Roland. *Two Ears of Corn: A Guide to People-Centred Agricultural Improvement*. Oklahoma City: World Neighbors, 1982.

Cairns, Earle E. *Christianity Through the Centuries: A History of the Christian Church*. Grand Rapids: Zondervan, 1967

Clinton, Robert J. *The Making of A Leader.* Colorado Springs: NavPress, 1988.

Cowart, John W. *People Whose Faith Got Them into Trouble: Stories of Costly Discipleship*. Downers Grove: IVP, 1990.

Dawson, John. *Conquérir nos villes pour Dieu (Taking Our Cities for God)*. Burtigny, Switerland: Youth With A Mission, 1991.

Elmer, Duane. *Cross-Cultural Conflict; Building Relationships for Effective Ministry*. Downers Grove: IVP, 1993.

Garrison, David. *Church Planting Movements*. Richmond, VA: Southern Baptist Convention, 2000.

Groupes Universitaires Bibliques. *Les communautés de maison – un espoir pour l'église*. Lausanne: Ligue pour la Lecture de la Bible, 1983.

Hamon, Bill. *Apostles, Prophets and the Coming Moves of God*. Santa Rosa Beach, FL: Christian International, 1997.

Hesselgrave, David J. *Communicating Christ Cross-Culturally: An Introduction to Missionary Communication*. Grand Rapids: Zondervan, 1991.

Hesselgrave, David J. *Planting Churches Cross-Culturally: A Guide for Home and Foreign Missions*. Grand Rapids: Baker, 1986.

Hodges, Melvin L. *A Guide to Church Planting*. Springfield, MO: Gospel Publishing House, 1976.

Johnstone, Patrick, and Jason Mandryk. *Operation World*. Carlisle, UK: Paternoster Lifestyle, 2001.

Johnstone, Patrick. *The Church is Bigger than You Think*. Pasadena: William Carey Library, 1998.

Käser, Lothar. *Fremde Kulturen - eine Einführung in die Ethnologie*. Bad Liebenzell: Verlag der Liebenzeller Mission, 1997.

Kuen, Alfred, ed. *Nouveau Dictionnaire Biblique*. St. Légier: Editions Emmaüs, 2002.

La Présidence Générale des Directions des Recherches Scientifiques Islamiques. *Le Saint Coran et la traduction en langue française du sens de ses versets*. Al-Madinah Al-Munawwarah, Arabie Saudite: Complexe du Roi Fahd, n.d.

Latourette, Kenneth S. *Missions Tomorrow*. New York: Harper, 1936.

Lingenfelter, Sherwood G., and Marvin K. Mayers. *Ministering Cross-Culturally*. Grand Rapids: Baker Academic, 1986.

Lingenfelter, Sherwood. *Transforming Culture: A Challenge for Christian Mission*. Grand Rapids: Baker, 1992.

Livingstone, Greg. *Planting Churches in Muslim Cities*. Grand Rapids: Baker, 1993.

Love, Rick. *Muslims, Magic and the Kingdom of God*. Pasadena: William Carey Library, 2000.

Maier, Gerhard. *Matthäus-Evangelium, 2. Teil, Edition C Bibelkommentar.* Holzgerlingen: Hänssler-Verlag, 1996.

Malek, Sobhi. *Islam: Challenge and Mandate*. Sobhi Malek, 2000.

McGavran, Donald A. *Understanding Church Growth*. Grand Rapids: Eerdmans, 1970.

Mears, Henrietta C. *Panorama du Nouveau Testament*. Miami: Edititions Vida, 1982.

Microsoft Encarta Encyclopedia 99. Redmond, WA: Microsoft Corporation, 1999.

Murphy, Joseph P. Carol Streams, IL: worldchristiandatabase.org, 2004.

Neighbour, Ralph W. *Where Do We Go from Here? A Guidebook for the Cell Group Church*. Houston: Touch Publications, 1990.

O'Donnell, Kelly, ed. *Missionary Care: Counting the Cost for World Evangelism*. Pasadena: William Carey Library, 1992.

O'Donnell, Kelly, ed. *Helping Missionaries Grow: Reading in Mental Health and Missions*. Pasadena: William Carey Library, 1988.

Parshall, Phil. *New Paths in Muslim Evangelism: Evangelical Approaches to Contextualization*. Grand Rapids: Baker, 1980.

Piper, John. *Let the Nations be Glad! The Supremacy of God in Missions*. Grand Rapids: Baker, 1995.

Pohl, Alfred. *Die Offenbarung des Johannes, 1. Teil Wuppertaler Studienbibel.* Wuppertal, Germany: R. Brockhaus Verlag, 1994.

Reeve, Robert. *Passion pour les nations*. Dijon, France: Editions Missionnaires Francophones, 2002.

Robb, John D. *Focus! The Power of People Group Thinking: A Practical Manual for Planning Effective Strategies to Reach the Unreached.* Monrovia: MARC, 1989.

Scoggins, Dick. *Planting House Churches in Networks*. Rev. ed., 1995.

Simson, Wolfgang. *Häuser, die die Welt verändern*. Rothrist, Switzerland: Koinonia-Verlag, 1999.

Stearns, Bill and Amy Stearns. *Catch the Vision 2000*. Minneapolis: Bethany House, 1991.

Taylor, William D., ed. *Too Valuable to Lose: Exploring the Causes and Cures of Missionary Attrition*. Pasadena: William Carey Library, 1997.

Thompson, Charles. *La Bible Thompson*. Miami: Editions Vida, 1991.

Tucker, Ruth A. *Aux extrémités de la terre, une histoire biographique des missions chrétiennes*. Miami: Editions Vida, 1989.

Uzodinma, Obed. *Mobilising Churches in Africa for Missions*. Basorun, Ibadan: Feyisetan Press, 2001.

Verwer, George. *Out of the Comfort Zone*. Carlisle, UK: Paternoster, 2000.

Wagner, C. Peter. *Acts of the Holy Spirit: A Modern Commentary on the Book of Acts*. Ventura: Regal Books, 2000.

Wagner, C. Peter. *Warfare Prayer*. Ventura: Regal Books, 1992.

Warren, Rick. *Kirche mit Vision (The Purpose Driven Church)*. Asslar: Projektion J. Verlag, 1998.

Wimber, John. *Allez... guérissez*. Rouen, France: Imprimerie A. Meyer, 1988.

Winter, Ralph D., and Steven C. Hawthorne, eds. *Perspectives on the World Christian Movement*. 3rd ed.. Pasadena: William Carey Library, 1999.

Yun, Brother, and Paul Hattaway. *The Heavenly Man*. London: Monarch Books, 2002.